We Hold
These Truths
TO BE
Self-Evident

12 Natural Laws of
Freedom, Progress, and Success

OLIVER DeMILLE

OBSTACLES
PRESS

First Edition, November 2013
10 9 8 7 6 5 4 3 2 1

Published by:

Obstaclés Press
4072 Market Place Dr.
Flint, MI 48507

www.life-leadership-home.com
www.life-leadership-home.ca

ISBN 978-0-9895763-8-3

Cover design and layout by Norm Williams, nwa-inc.com

Printed in the United States of America

The only reliable basis for sound government and just human relations is Natural Law.
—W. Cleon Skousen

CONTENTS

ACKNOWLEDGMENTS

Many people are involved in preparing any book and getting it ready for its readers. I am so grateful to all who have helped this project, especially the entire team at Obstaclés Press. In addition, three people went far beyond the typical contribution, and without them, this book would not have been possible. Orrin Woodward gave ongoing feedback throughout the writing of this book, and in fact he contributed so many ideas and suggestions that he could easily have been a coauthor. His deep insight has been truly invaluable. Very special thanks to Shanon Brooks, president of Monticello College, who first suggested to me the idea of a book on natural law and how this is deeply needed in our society. He pointed out that college students need a book on natural law that helps them tackle this important topic; there are many deep works on the subject, but few that introduce its huge relevance to society. In fact, as he noted, natural law is vital and essential to freedom, and all free citizens—not just students—need to understand it in depth. And thanks to Emma Cox, whose excellent research, suggestions, ideas, and willingness to argue for important points significantly improved this book.

INTRODUCTION

By Orrin Woodward

I t's no secret that America is losing its freedoms, but few have any idea where to begin in the effort to restore them. In fact, most people who are concerned about America spend most of their time ranting and raving against particular parties or individuals, leaving the deep-rooted issues unquestioned, unaddressed, and thereby unresolved.

America was founded upon the self-evident principles and inalienable rights captured in its founding documents: the Declaration of Independence, the Articles of Confederation, and the US Constitution. Unfortunately, however, few read these documents, and fewer still comprehend the vital message communicated within them.

Oliver DeMille's new book explains these self-evident principles in such clear and concise language that any adult can grasp their meaning. Those who truly want to make a difference in the world must first make a difference in themselves by disciplining themselves to look past the surface waves and into the deeper movements of the underlying tide.

This is exactly what Oliver has done in this groundbreaking introduction to natural law. Many people ask me what they can do to make a difference. My answer is always the same, namely, educate yourself by reading books from the greatest minds discussing the greatest thoughts in any area where you desire to help. All true change begins when hunger leads to wisdom—which leads to proper actions and finally results.

Unfortunately, today we live in a microwave age where people want instant results without doing the heavy lifting required to gain wisdom. Oliver refuses to cater to the "dumbing down" culture prevalent in our society today; instead, he is "smarting up" people who read his numerous books and articles about the true meaning of liberty and freedom.

There simply is no substitute for each person learning the truths behind the founding of America. Knowing what they did right and what they did wrong is essential if we want to keep the good and change the bad. But how can this be done if no one reads, thinks, or applies these natural principles into his or her life?

This, in my opinion, is the greatest challenge facing America. Too few seem willing to set aside the time needed to acquire what Oliver would term a "Thomas Jefferson Education."

For instance, when America was on the verge of declaring independence and breaking away from the British Empire, Edmund Burke rose and told the British Parliament that the American colonists were leading a revolution because of one thing: they understood the law.

Today, few would have any idea what Burke was referring to, but in 1775, the Americans did. Colonial leaders were avid students of government, society, and natural law through extensive study of Greco-Roman, Judeo-Christian, and Anglo-Saxon history.

Burke told Parliament that nearly all Americans read the great classics on these topics, and then he said:

> This study renders men acute, inquisitive, dexterous, prompt in attack, ready in defense, full of resources. In other countries, the people, more simple, and of a less [brilliant] caste, judge of an ill principle in government only by an actual grievance; here they anticipate the evil, and judge of the pressure of the grievance by the badness of the principle. They [foresee] misgovernment at a distance; and snuff the approach of tyranny in every tainted breeze.

The Americans, in other words, knew their history and the principles of freedom and could not be fooled by the machinations of a tyrannous king and parliament.

Specifically, Americans understood the principles of law (which Blackstone and many of the founders called "the law of nature" or "natural law") that make freedom work. They understood the twelve principles of natural law outlined in this book.

Because of this understanding, they knew when freedom was spreading and when it was under attack. Unless we have a similar understanding, we can never have the same freedoms—because we won't even know what to aim for.

America's founders ensured their freedoms because they understood them. Today, America is losing its freedoms because it does not understand them. Dismally ignorant of our past, many American citizens vote for the chains that bind us tighter every year. Many Canadians and other people in historically free nations do the same.

This must end. Toward that end, my good friend and coauthor of the *New York Times* bestseller *LeaderShift* wrote this book. As the people educate themselves on the twelve laws, it will become clear when the president, Congress, the Supreme Court, or anyone else is violating our freedoms. To fix America, in other words, people must learn and apply these twelve laws. For without them, no solution is forthcoming.

NATURAL LAW MATTERS

"I know natural law is important," he said. "I really love reading about freedom and the founding fathers, and natural law was an essential part of the American founding and of freedom through history. But why would an average person care about it?"

I stroked my chin as I considered the question. "Well, for starters, natural law is the basis of the Declaration of Independence. When Jefferson wrote that we hold these truths to be self-evident, what specifically were the self-evident truths he thought were so important?"

"Natural laws," he affirmed, "like inalienable rights to life, liberty, and the pursuit of happiness. I get that. But how is this relevant to most people? How does it directly impact their daily lives?"

"Wow. That's a fantastic question." I stood and began pacing as I talked. "The thing is, hardly *anything* has more direct impact on everybody's daily life than natural law. Hardly *anything*..."

He sat forward in his chair and said intently, "That's the passion I'm looking for. I can feel it when you say it that way. You obviously care deeply about this, and so do I. But for most people, natural law is just some old phrase from a college textbook. Why should anyone feel as passionately about this as we do?"

Natural law was an essential part of the American founding and of freedom through history.

"Because natural law is the most important issue right now in American politics," I said, "and for that matter, in the politics of Canada, Europe, and every other nation in the free world. If people only knew just how important it is. . . ." I paused to catch my breath. Then I turned and looked him directly in the eyes and said, "Nothing, absolutely *nothing*, has as much impact on the daily lives of every modern person as natural law."

"Why?" He smiled and sat back in his seat.

I followed his lead and smiled widely. "Why?" I asked. "Okay, here's why. Because the operating principle of the modern United States government is that the federal government is the supreme being in the universe."

"The *supreme being*?" he asked skeptically.

"Yes, the supreme being. Or call it the 'most powerful being' if you prefer. The government today acts on the assumption that it is the most powerful thing in the universe." I could see that he was still skeptical, and I took a deep breath. Then in a more relaxed posture, I said, "Okay, just follow me for a minute.

"What if the government's basic operating principle was that it was the most powerful entity in the world? What if those who led it felt they were the most powerful people anywhere on Earth? Wouldn't they feel that if anything bad happened in the world, they should do something about it?

"After all, if you're the supreme being, don't you want to be a good supreme being? Caring? Loving? Helping those in need? Well, that's the driving force of modern government. It is operating on the belief that it should fix every problem, right every wrong, and never allow any pain or suffering in the world—because if it doesn't fix things, who will?

"So, if you believe that government is the last hope to fix the world's problems, you think government should do everything it can to solve every problem. And if it doesn't have the resources or money or personnel to fix everything, it should find a way to raise taxes and borrow money and increase its regulations in order to get all the power it needs.

"If you truly, deeply felt this way, you would do whatever you could to give the government more and more power, to get it involved in every detail of every person's life, both in the United States and around the world.

"And you wouldn't limit it to things here in North America. If you felt that Washington was the most powerful government on the globe, and the last hope for helping people everywhere, you would use America's power to try to intervene and fix all the problems everywhere in the world. And you'd be frustrated if there was any place or anything you couldn't intervene in.

"You would see the presidency as the most powerful job in Washington, so the White House would be the supreme power in the world, and you would dedicate your life to helping Washington get as much power as possible and using it to get more and more involved in every person's life and putting an end to every bit of human pain, suffering, or need.

"And you wouldn't care about debts, deficits, budgets, or overspending, because these would just be roadblocks to fixing the world. You'd basically ignore these things and spend as much as you could get away with. And then you'd find ways to spend even more."

He nodded slowly, taking it all in.

"You wouldn't give up no matter what," I continued. "Year after year, decade after decade, you would push to give more money and power to government and have government more involved in every facet of people's lives. You would see it as your highest duty and your mission in life. And anyone who stood against it, who argued for limited government or constitutional rights or anything else, what would you think of them?

"You would consider them ignorant at best," I said, "or at worst, you would see them as enemies of progress and everything that is decent and good. You'd keep reminding yourself that there is suffering in the world and government is the only real solution.

> *Government just keeps growing, and it will continue to grow as long as the leadership principle of modern government is that there is no higher power than government and its purpose is to fix everything possible.*

"And you would ignore them as much as possible and surround yourself with 'enlightened' people and media who agree with you that if government doesn't fix the problems and end all suffering, nobody is going to do it."

"But it's not true," he said. "Government isn't the supreme being."

"You're right," I nodded. "But for the last eighty years this has increasingly become the operating principle of Washington DC, the prime directive of the US government. And it is getting worse with each passing decade."

"But government hasn't even come close to removing all suffering in America or the world," he said.

"But that hasn't stopped it from trying," I noted. "In fact, almost every president since the end of World War II has followed the pattern of drastically growing the US government, increasing taxes and power, and doing more and more to try to fix every problem and right every wrong.

"Presidents of both parties have done it. A few have given lip service to slowing the growth of government or even rolling it back a little, but none have actually done it. Government spending has grown under every president since 1930. Government just keeps growing, and it will continue to grow as long as the leadership principle of modern government is that there is no higher power than government and its purpose is to fix everything possible—as long as we ignore the idea that God rules in human affairs."

He sat forward again in his seat and moved the book from his lap to the coffee table. "It sounds like a religion of government. And as long as the nation's choices are based on this view, we'll never fix Washington or slow the loss of freedom."

"Oh, everyone's careful never to use words that sound religious in any way." I continued pacing. "But the belief remains that government is the most powerful entity in the world and that it should fix every problem. Many people in Washington have stopped believing the national motto 'In God We Trust'; now it's become 'In Government We Trust.'"

"And the idea is that if it doesn't have the power to fix a problem, it should just print more money or raise taxes or borrow it," he affirmed. "That's why socialism grows, no matter who wins elections. Nobody uses the word *socialism* anymore, but that's still what it is. Government just keeps growing, trying to fix every problem."

I sat down. "Yes, and it will keep growing until all our freedoms are lost and government regulates everything. We are already on track for this right now, and every year this growth of government has more and more impact on the daily lives of every person and family in the free world."

"Nothing's going to stop this agenda, is it?" he asked, sighing.

"Nothing except natural law," I said.

"Exactly," he responded with renewed excitement, "because natural law says that the federal government isn't the highest power in the world. And also because natural law has the ability to gain the support of both religious believers and those with a secular view."

I leaned forward. "The one thing standing in the way of modern government taking over every part of our lives is natural law. This is because natural law takes the belief in government as the supreme being and cuts it off at the knees.

Whether natural law or bigger government wins this battle will have more impact on all our daily lives than pretty much anything else in the world.

"The great historian Will Durant quoted Solon as saying that a good government occurs 'when the people obey the rulers and the rulers obey the laws.' But this only happens when the laws are based on natural laws that are higher than humankind's laws."

I stood again and spoke with feeling: "*Nobody* who understands natural law will believe that Washington is the great hope of the world, or that government must fix everything, or that government needs more resources and power.

"*Everybody* who really understands natural law will see that government has become much too big and that its growth is actually causing more problems than it solves," I said emphatically.

"And *everyone* who understands natural law will know that if we continue on this path, we're going to see America decline and fall in the decades ahead."

He stood and walked to stand beside me at the window. We looked down on the lake and the green of the forest that surrounded the water. The wind swayed the trees slightly, and small waves rippled across the lake. The view from his Michigan office was gorgeous.

He turned and said, "We've got to teach natural law, and we can't water it down or make it a shallow book. It's got to be deep, so the readers really do understand natural law. And we've got to help them see just how important it is."

"Yes," I said, nodding, "because whether natural law or bigger government wins this battle will have more impact on all our daily lives than pretty much anything else in the world—literally."

He went back to his chair and reached for the book on the coffee table. He opened it to a turned-down page. After scanning for a moment, he looked up and said, "One thing still bothers me, though. In some of the books I read, natural law is portrayed as the same thing as God's law or revealed law, but in other books, it is defined as a secularist alternative to revelation, or something to be used against God's law. Which is the correct definition?"

"Unfortunately, the phrase *natural law* has been used by a number of different people through history," I said, "and many have defined it their own way. So you have to read the definition each person gives it to know what they're saying. But the traditional definition is simply law that is higher than manmade laws or governments, meaning higher laws that even governments have to follow."

I continued. "For religious people through history, revealed law has been the higher law that all should follow, while unbelievers followed the teachings of Aristotle, Cicero, the Stoics, and other great philosophers who taught that reason was the source of understanding laws that are higher than humans.

"In the Middle Ages, these two streams of thought came together, teaching that there are higher laws above humans. In modern times, natural law includes all laws that are above humankind, including revealed law and scientific law, and that's the only definition I'll use in the book because that's the natural law that will win over the modern belief in government as the supreme being."

"Agreed." He nodded and then sat quietly and mulled over the ideas for a few moments.

"Well," he said thoughtfully, "do you really think natural law can win this battle? Government has just grown too big, and the idea that government is the greatest power in the world has just become too entrenched. I don't see how we can stop government from growing and growing, eventually forcing itself into every part of our lives and homes and continually hacking away at our freedoms."

This is the great battle of our time.

He paused, closed the book, and sat back in his chair. "I'm an optimist, and I'm also a realist. Do you think we can win?"

I grinned. "You like asking these Socratic questions, don't you? I mean, you already know the answers, but you ask anyway, just to make me think."

He laughed; then his face grew serious. "But can we win?"

I immediately responded, "I believe we were *born* to win. That's who we *are*—not just you and me, but thousands of people in this generation. This is the great battle of our time. And, yes, we're going to win. We might win soon enough to stave off a crash, or we might win after a big crash, but we're going to win. Failure is not an option."

"Excellent," he said firmly. "You and I are in the same place on this. I think you're right to write this book. It is desperately needed in our world, and the sooner the better." He paused, and we both reflected.

"There is only one way we can win," he mused. "Do you know what it is?"

"More Socratic questioning?" We both laughed. Then I pondered and replied, "We will only win if the people in our generation come to really understand natural law. Otherwise, the focus will continue to be on bigger and bigger government, no matter what."

He nodded. "The future of freedom and prosperity depends on millions of us understanding natural law and the proper role of government."

CHAPTER 1

THE LAW OF SUPREMACY

NATURAL LAW, NOT MANMADE LAW, IS SUPREME;
IT IS THE BASIS OF ALL FREEDOM AND SUCCESS, AND
ALL MANMADE CONSTITUTIONS AND LAWS MUST ADHERE
TO NATURAL LAW OR FREEDOM WILL DECREASE.

Sir William Blackstone, the founder of modern law, said, "[T]he law of nature . . . is binding over all the globe, in all countries at all times. No human laws are of any validity, if contrary to this; and such of them as are valid, derive all their authority . . . from this." This understanding is the foundation of all good laws and free society.

There are laws that are higher than manmade laws. Such laws are called natural law, and they are the basis of all freedom and all success. This is what Jefferson was referring to when he wrote, "We hold these truths to be self-evident . . ." When we violate natural law—as individuals, organizations, governments, or nations—there are negative consequences.

Many people have lost this understanding in modern times, and it is the biggest challenge in our current world because only the application of true principles can fix our nations and lead to real progress. Yet most people haven't given any thought to just how significant natural law really is.

Two Concrete Examples

The idea of natural law—laws above humanity—is self-evident. For example, if a congress or parliament becomes deeply concerned that too many broken bones are caused by people falling from ladders and passes a law that from now on, any person falling off a ladder will gently float to the earth and land without harmful impact, most people would consider such a law absurd. Moreover, it wouldn't work. The law of gravity is higher than, and supersedes, any manmade law.

When we violate natural law—as individuals, organizations, governments, or nations—there are negative consequences.

A critic of natural law might argue: "But the legislators who promoted such a law had very good intentions. After all, a lot of people get hurt falling off ladders." No matter how true this is, the law of gravity still doesn't submit itself to man's laws.

Likewise, if the legislature of Kansas feels deep concern for the frustration of math students trying to use the symbol π to work geometrical calculations and, in an effort to lessen their workload, votes to change the value of π from 3.1416 to a nice, even 3, some might applaud their concern for the youth of their state. But mathematical laws, like the law of gravity and other scientific laws, don't follow manmade laws, however well-intentioned they may be.

Moral or Political Laws

There are laws that are higher than humans. Some are scientific, others are mathematical, and still others are moral or political. Among such laws, Jefferson said, are these: all men (in Jefferson's time, women were, unfortunately, essentially considered property controlled by their fathers or husbands, so it likely did not occur to him to include women in his statement) are created equal, all men are endowed by their creator with inalienable rights that no government can take away without negative consequences, and among these inalienable rights are life, liberty, property (which Jefferson wrote in an early draft of the Declaration of Independence), and the pursuit of happiness.

These are natural laws of the political type, and they are just as real and lasting as the scientific and mathematical laws of the universe. For example, if a government allows slavery, it guarantees major negative consequences in the future because it is breaking natural law.

All natural laws are above humans, and manmade laws are only good to the extent that they harmonize with natural law.

The Roman statesman Cicero, who was executed by the government for opposing tyranny, wrote: "But the most foolish notion of all is the belief that everything is just which is found in the customs or laws of nations. . . . What of the many deadly, the many pestilential statutes which nations put into force. These no more deserve to be called laws than the rules a band of robbers might pass in their assembly."[1]

Note what Cicero called the most foolish idea of all: the belief that manmade laws can break natural law.

The first chief justice of the US Supreme Court, John Marshall, said that law must always be based on true natural law,[2] and Alexander Hamilton taught the same thing in *Federalist* 31 and 78.[3] The American founding generation held that all laws must be in keeping with natural law.[4]

Four Types of Laws

Historically, there are four major types of law:

1. Scriptural laws taught by world religions and moral leaders (for example, the Ten Commandments)

2. Scientific, mathematical, and moral laws that are above humankind (for example, gravity)

3. Laws of nations that countries must follow in dealing with each other or suffer negative natural consequences (for example, nations that attack other nations for plunder will suffer increased corruption of their home government and society)

4. Manmade laws (for example, vehicles must stop at a posted stop sign or their drivers are subject to a fine)

The first three are all laws that are above humans, and together they are called natural law. If nations or individuals break them, there are inevitable natural consequences, and manmade laws cannot undo such consequences.

The Need for Change

Natural law provides solutions to many of our most pressing modern challenges. Learning about natural law will bring a much-needed refocus on our founding principles. It will show conservatives and liberals where both sides went wrong, while reaffirming the things we got right.

Just as understanding the law of gravity allowed scientists and inventors to discover the law of lift and learn to fly, a return to the laws of nature will yield new wisdom and increased abilities to improve our political institutions, communities, business leadership, and nations.

Our governments need many revisions, and we will never fix our biggest national problems until we understand their root causes. Too much in our modern politics deals primarily with symptoms rather than real causes. The solutions to our greatest concerns will only come from true principles. Such principles are the very DNA, the building blocks and substance, of natural law.

Once we understand natural law, the solutions to our problems will be clear. They won't necessarily be easy, but we will at the very least understand what we need to do to heal our nations and get back on the path of progress. Without a clear understanding of natural law, our problems will continue to fester and spin out of control.

Unless more people once again understand natural law, the idea that government is the supreme being in the world and must continue to grow and grow and grow will only gain more support. We'll never fix runaway government without a widespread understanding of natural law.

Natural law is powerful because we are living with its consequences every day, just as we do with gravity or mathematical laws. Even an isolated tribe somewhere in the jungle that has never learned the law of gravity is still living under it, just as the millions of people who don't understand natural law are still impacted by its effects. Only when we understand the higher laws and use them to our advantage can we fix our problems and create the future of progress and success that we want.

For example, just as understanding the law of gravity allowed scientists and inventors to discover the law of lift and learn to fly, a return to the laws of nature will yield new wisdom and increased abilities to improve our political institutions, communities, business leadership, and nations.

Success always comes from effectively applying true principles. This works for individuals and companies and also for governments. Failures and decline come when we don't apply such principles. Natural law is the combination of all true principles.

It isn't the purpose of this book to list every natural law in the universe. But a few, an amazing few, are being widely broken or ignored by free nations in the world today, causing the negative results we watch on the nightly news. It is time to understand these natural laws, and it is time to do something about them.

Once we clearly know what they are, we will be empowered to lead real change in our world.

This book will introduce twelve natural laws that will make all the difference because all are being violated by modern governments and societies, and many of the negatives we face in our world are the natural consequences of this.

We will never fix our major national problems or get our society back on track as long as we are breaking these twelve laws, and we can't do much about them if we don't understand them.

Of course, there are more than just twelve natural laws, but these twelve are the ones that are hurting our society most right now and holding it back from real progress.

The first of the twelve is the law of supremacy, which simply states that natural law (including both God's laws and scientific laws of the universe) is supreme and above all manmade laws and that our manmade laws and governments are struggling because many of them are breaking natural law.

Natural law is real, whether we know about it or not, and like gravity, it is acting upon us every minute of every day. By learning the basics of the twelve natural laws covered in this book, we will finally understand what is happening in our political world and what can effectively be done about it. Such wisdom is long overdue.

We will never fix our major national problems or get our society back on track as long as we are breaking these twelve laws, and we can't do much about them if we don't understand them.

CHAPTER 2

THE LAW OF AUTHORITY

IN FREE SOCIETIES,
ALL GOVERNMENT POWER COMES FROM THE PEOPLE.

T he great medieval philosopher William of Occam, who is most famous in scientific circles as the inventor of Occam's Razor (which posits that the simplest answer is often correct), said, "What touches all should be approved by all."[1] He was speaking directly of free government.

This principle was also taught by the father of natural law, or, more accurately, the great *promoter* of natural law, Samuel von Pufendorf. The American founders were close students of Pufendorf's writings because his additions to the understanding of natural law and how it works in society were vital in the creation of truly free government.

Of course, believers correctly point out that God is the true author and father of natural law, and unbelievers have long referred to nature as the ultimate author of natural law. At different times in history, various thinkers have been called the father of natural law, including Aristotle, Cicero, Thomas Aquinas, and Hugo Grotius.

Each of these men made major contributions in humanity's discovery of natural law. Aristotle taught that natural law is real, that it is above manmade governments and laws, and that all human laws are only good to the extent that they conform to natural law.

Cicero reinforced these ideas and added the focus that God or nature endowed humankind with reason as a natural gift that allows all people to consider, understand, and apply natural law.

Aquinas formalized the natural law philosophy by discussing it in detail and considering it from many different angles, and he added to our understanding of natural law with the idea that the greatest law is to do good and avoid evil. Of course, this had been clearly taught by both Socrates and Jesus Christ centuries before.

Hugo Grotius was the first to effectively emphasize the direct application of natural law into the actual policies of manmade laws and governments. This transition from theory to practical implementation in government laid the foundation for the spread of natural law across the free world.

Samuel Pufendorf stood on the shoulders of these greats in his writings between 1650 and 1694. He added two major principles to our understanding of natural law, and he was frequently quoted by Locke, Blackstone, and Montesquieu, the three most influential thinkers (the one thing that wielded greater influence than the works of these men was the Bible) in the American founding era, as well as by Jefferson, Hamilton, Madison, and many other American founding thinkers and leaders.

Of the People...

Pufendorf's first major contribution, beyond affirming the basics of natural law that had been taught by earlier thinkers, was the fundamental relationship between natural law and human beings, and between humans and their governments.[2] To begin with, there are two kinds of manmade laws/governments: (1) those that are free and (2) those that are not free.

> *Manmade government is only legitimate or legal, meaning that it is in keeping with natural law, if it is established and continues to operate with the consent of the governed.*

A free government receives its power from the people and serves with the consent of the people. Any other type of government is not free because the people are forced to follow it. And only free government operates in accordance with natural law, meaning that government by force, enslavement, or any claim to authority other than the consent of the majority of the people is actually illegitimate.

This means that every such government is in conflict with natural law, and it will inevitably face negative consequences unless it changes and gets back in line with natural law. This is the law of authority, also called the law of legitimacy.

Manmade government is only legitimate or legal, meaning that it is in keeping with natural law, if it is established and continues to operate with the consent of the governed. Otherwise it has no true authority. It may rule by might, but its authority is illegitimate.

This view was, of course, foundational for the American Revolution, and it was strongly opposed by most of the European monarchies and aristocracies, who felt they had a divine right to rule, regardless of the consent of the governed.[3]

Pufendorf outlined the reasons behind this natural law, as well as the reasons for many other natural laws that are vital to free society. Specifically, he taught the following natural laws:[4]

- A person must do no wrong to another peson.

- "Wrong" is anything a person has no natural right to do to another.

- This protection from a wrong is called a "right."

- The wrongs include murder, wounding, striking, rape, theft, fraud, violence, slur, attack on a reputation, harm, damage, breaking a contract that was willingly joined, and not taking care of one's spouse or children.

- The rights include life, liberty, ownership of property, and freedom to pursue one's desires (as long as no wrongs are committed in the process).

> *The purpose of government is to maintain equal liberty for all people.*

This is the basic foundation of freedom.

The Reason for Government

Pufendorf also provided the natural law framework for the role of government, as follows:[5]

- Any person wronging another naturally forfeits some of his or her own rights until just reparations are made to the victim.

- Other people should hold the person who caused the damage accountable for reparations.

- A person who harms by chance or accident, through no fault of his or her own, should not be held to reparations by the victim or by others—but he or she may hold him- or herself accountable for the reparation.

- Another person (not the harmer or the victim) may act as an intermediary and make reparation to the victim on behalf of the one who did the harm.

- When reparation is made, the person harmed and all others should give the person who caused the harm a pardon (forgiveness).

- Any requirement of reparations beyond the just level of the harm, after the harmer should be pardoned, is called revenge and is itself a new harm or wrong.

- All men and women are equal before the natural law and should treat each other equally; any violation of this is a harm.

- Equality means that all people have different strengths and weaknesses, but they have equal liberty before natural law.

Thus, the purpose of government is to maintain equal liberty for all people and to right wrongs as a group of citizens when a person who does harm refuses to make just reparation to a victim.

The Foundations of Government

Pufendorf continued, expounding on how these basics become a functioning government:[6]

- Every man and woman should stand and take action to maintain equal liberty for every person.

- Any failure to take action to maintain equal liberty for all is a harm against those who lose freedom, and such a harm will require reparation from every person who doesn't actively stop the harm.

- Individuals should join in alliance with others to accomplish this protection of equal freedom.

- If the threat to equal freedom comes from a foreign power, rather than a local person committing harm, the same principles apply.

In short, government is in keeping with natural law when it consists of the people willingly working together to do what natural morality requires them to do as their duty. Such action always involves protecting natural, inalienable rights.

This was Pufendorf's first great contribution to human understanding of natural law. When no government exists, there are still right and wrong behaviors, and it is each person's duty to do right and avoid wrong. When a person does wrong in a way that harms another, he or she must make just reparation to the person harmed.

This is all simple, basic natural law. It is what C. S. Lewis called "fair" and what Thomas Paine called "common sense." When a person harms another and refuses to make fair reparation, other people should hold the perpetrator accountable to do the right thing. This is the beginning of manmade law.

When more is needed, when a group of people is necessary to hold a perpetrator accountable or to keep a foreign attacker from violating the rights of the people, the people can choose to band together to ensure that justice is done and freedom is protected. This is the beginning of manmade government.

Manmade governments are legal if they exist for these reasons, as long as they have the consent of the people they govern. This makes them free and also legitimate.

If one or more of these requirements are not met, the government is illegitimate and will not be or remain free. When this occurs, as Jefferson famously wrote, it is the right, and duty, of the people to alter or abolish this government and replace it as necessary to establish a free and legitimate government.[7]

In short, governments work for the people and answer to the people, not vice versa. This is an essential law of freedom, and any government that doesn't follow this law will not remain free.

CHAPTER 3

The Law of Limits

FREE GOVERNMENTS ONLY SUCCEED WHEN THEY ARE
STRONG AND VIGOROUS, AND FREEDOM ONLY LASTS
IF THEIR POWER IS EFFECTIVELY LIMITED.

James Madison and Alexander Hamilton summarized Pufendorf's natural law teachings in the *Federalist* papers.[1] First, manmade government is necessary in order to protect equality before
natural law, known as inalienable rights.

Second, it must protect the inalienable rights of the people from
criminals and also from foreign attackers. This is why government
exists.

Third, in order to accomplish this
effectively, government must be both
strong and vigorous. The words *vigor*
and *vigorous* are used thirteen times
in the *Federalist* papers to describe the
type of government that is needed.

> *If government is too
> vigorous, there is no
> freedom. If government isn't
> vigorous enough, liberty is
> lost to foreign aggression.*

Without a vigorous government,
one that actively focuses on protecting equal rights, there will be
numerous abuses of inalienable rights, and freedom will decrease and
eventually be lost. Madison wrote that "the vigor of government is
essential to the security of liberty."[2]

Note that vigor is necessary to stop chaos, but there must be checks
on government to keep it from becoming corrupt and abusive, and the
more vigorous the government, the more powerful the checks must
be in order to ensure liberty. If government is too vigorous, there is
no freedom. If government isn't vigorous enough, liberty is lost to

foreign aggression. In history, both extremes (too much vigor and too much chaos) have occurred.

For example, Greece failed because it was too chaotic; the Greek states refused to unite or even cooperate enough, so they fell to their enemies (particularly Persia, Macedon, and later Rome). On the opposite extreme, the Roman government was too vigorous, eventually swallowing up the rights of the people and declining from a freedom-loving republic into a totalitarian empire. The American framers wrote extensively about this needed balance between vigorous government and effective checks on all government powers.[3]

The Problem and the Solution

Fourth, government is power, and unfortunately power is dangerous to liberty. Thus, the very power and vigor of government that effectively protect inalienable rights will inevitably be used by some government officials to stop protecting rights and do other things that government shouldn't do.

Some of these are bad things, which the people will usually see and can stop if they so choose. But others are good things, which most people will be tempted to allow. Whatever government effort is focused on anything other than protecting inalienable rights will reduce the vigor of government in protecting freedoms. It will also cause a decrease of freedom immediately and a loss of all freedom over time.

> *Whatever government effort is focused on anything other than protecting inalienable rights will reduce the vigor of government in protecting freedoms.*

Periodically, as the economist Murray Rothbard pointed out, government reaches a point that it considers itself a monopoly of force, refusing to let individual citizens even defend themselves; they are instead expected to leave all protection to government. When governments get to this point, freedom is deeply in jeopardy. Freedom is inalienable, as the Declaration of Independence declares, and people have the right to protect themselves. In fact, government gets this power directly from the people.

So when government becomes a monopoly of force, it is an enemy of freedom. Sadly, as Rothbard mentioned, this happens to more governments than not.

Fifth, therefore, government must be limited. And the best way to limit it is by what the framers called "auxiliary precautions." The founders wrote seven of the *Federalist* papers specifically on the auxiliary precautions, the measures that limit government so that it will focus on its real purpose: to protect inalienable rights.[4]

The auxiliary precautions include the following:

1. Separations of power between the legislative, executive, and judicial branches of government

2. Separations of power between the spending (House of Representatives) and governing (Senate) houses of Congress

3. Separations of power between the local, state, and federal levels of executive institutions of government

4. Separations of power between the local, state, and federal levels of legislative institutions of government

5. Separations of power between the local, state, and federal levels of judicial institutions of government

6. Checks between all of these institutions, branches, and levels of government

7. Balances between all of these institutions, branches, and levels of government

8. Periodic and frequent elections

9. A written constitution that outlines these limits

10. A written constitution requiring ratification by the people of a super-majority of the states

11. A written constitution that outlines the exact powers of government

12. A written constitution that clearly says that the government shall have no additional powers

13. Constitutional limits on who can run for office, by age and where they live

14. A constitutional requirement of a federal form of government where each state has its own sovereignty

15. A requirement that the president be elected by the representatives of all the states in an electoral college so that a few states with huge populations don't elect all the presidents regardless of small-state desires

These might seem too tedious for modern readers, but the founding generation considered these precautions vital for freedom. If we've reached a point where readers won't study these things, we have reached a place where we will lose our freedoms—because freedom only lasts when the regular people study it and understand it in depth. Freedom is based on natural law, period.

James Madison pointed out in *Federalist* 31 that all good laws must be based on natural law and that without this, manmade law is flawed.

All these precautions were written into the United States Constitution because the framers understood the law of authority, that natural law is the template for all good manmade law, and that the only good, legal, and free governments are those with the original and ongoing consent of the majority of those governed.

For America to decline, some or many of these auxiliary precautions must be weakened. In fact, in our time, all fifteen of these special protections of freedom are weaker than they were even fifty years ago.

Widespread Education Vital
for Freedom

The founding generation also understood that the people won't be able to rightly consent to a government unless they clearly understand it. Thus, widespread education is essential to the maintenance of freedom.

The framers took as their models two of the freest nations in history: the ancient Israelites and the Anglo-Saxons. These two societies had much in common; for example, the government was made up of a nation of free citizens, the whole legal system was based on ensuring just reparation to victims of crime, all problems were solved at the lowest possible level of government, all those accused were considered innocent until proven guilty, and no slavery was allowed, among other things.[5]

But all this was based on the fact that in order to become an adult member of the society, a young person had to study and know the entire law by heart and consent to entering and upholding the laws of the nation.[6]

The American founding generation took this concept of widespread education to heart. Pufendorf had noted that educating one's children was a fundamental duty of any parent.[7] John Adams wrote at length on the importance of educating the citizens in a free

When senators, CEOs, judges, and presidents have a different kind and level of education than the regular people, the system is an aristocracy.

society,[8] and Tocqueville noted the level of American education as one of the best and most surprising characteristics of the young nation. Tocqueville wrote in *Democracy in America*:

> [An American's] language will become as clear and precise as his thoughts. He will inform you what his rights are and by what means he exercises them; he will be able to point out the customs which obtain in the political world. You will find that

he is well acquainted with the rules of administration, and that he is familiar with the mechanism of the laws. . . .

The American learns to know the laws by participating in the act of legislation; and he takes a lesson in the forms of government from governing. The great work of society is ever going on before his eyes, and, as it were, under his hands.

In the United States, politics are the end aim of education.[9]

When Tocqueville said that the great work of society is ever going on before the American's eyes, he meant that the regular citizens were broadly read and actively kept track of history and current events. This is not the basic literacy aimed for by most modern schools, although literacy is certainly important, but rather the deep education of a political leader.

Indeed, until the 1930s and the spread of the conveyor-belt approach to education, nearly all citizens were expected to have, and the majority did have, an education equal to that of their top business and political leaders. When senators, CEOs, judges, and presidents have a different kind and level of education than the regular people, the system is an aristocracy.

The law of authority or the law of legitimacy says that in free societies, all governmental powers come from the people and by their consent. This was true in the founding of America and most other nations in the free world, but unless it remains true, freedom will be lost. Education—especially the lifelong pursuit of free people reading the great classics and other important books—is central to maintaining freedom that endures.

Only widespread education creates the environment where the people preserve a government that is simultaneously strong, vigorous, and effectively limited. This balance between vigor and limits is the key to lasting freedom in any society.

CHAPTER 4

THE LAW OF DELEGATION

THE PEOPLE MAY NOT DELEGATE TO GOVERNMENT ANY POWER
THEY DO NOT POSSESS BY NATURAL LAW.

The great medieval Spanish thinker Francisco Suárez taught, "In the nature of things all men are born free, so that, consequently, no person has political jurisdiction over another."[1] In the same vein, Samuel Pufendorf's second major contribution to humanity's understanding of natural law is an obvious point: No person can give away something he or she doesn't possess.

Put in another light, one cannot delegate a role or responsibility that one does not have to begin with, and one cannot bestow a gift, privilege, or right that one does not own. Amazingly, this self-evident truth has been misunderstood or ignored by almost all government officials in history.

Even more surprising, many citizens have also had a difficult time understanding it. There are two main reasons for this difficulty. First, people tend to differentiate in their minds between what one person can morally do and what a large group of people can morally do.

For example, according to natural law, if a person harms another through theft, society should require the thief to make fair reparation by paying back the victim. This is where government comes in. But imagine that Bob just wants more money, sees that Tom has a lot, and decides to get people to help him take some of Tom's money.

Obviously, nobody should work together to force Tom to pay money to Bob under such circumstances.

What if indigent Bob broke into Tom's house and took money? Obviously, Bob would be in trouble with the law—natural and manmade. What if he tried to get the neighborhood to go into Tom's house and take the money against Tom's will? The fact that Tom is wealthy doesn't mean people get to come take his stuff.

What if Bob gets a police officer or city official or even the mayor to break in and take it? What if he becomes a policeman, puts on his uniform, and then takes it? The act is still theft.

> *No person can give away something he or she doesn't possess.*

So far, this is clear common sense. If Bob prints posters and campaigns to force Tom to pay him money, not for a harm or to fulfill a contract but simply because Bob has less money than Tom and really wants some of Tom's money, few people will support Bob in this obvious attempt to steal.

Even if Bob can convince three, four, or five people to support him, most citizens will still consider this a ridiculous plan. Most will remain skeptical even if Bob persuades three hundred or three thousand to back his plan. But something amazing happens as Bob gains more supporters. In fact, at some point, if Bob's project keeps gaining popularity, it will eventually tip the scales in a way that alters how most people look at it.

If Bob gains enough support, the majority will stop being skeptical, will stop arguing that Bob has no right to Tom's money, and will begin to believe that Tom really should stop being so greedy and shell out for Bob's wants.

This subtle shift can occur even if Bob never mentions government or elections, but it will happen more quickly and people will be more passionately supportive of Bob's plan if he uses government terms, parties, policies, and media.

If the group becomes large enough that it is faceless, people often switch to a mob mentality, where they rationalize that big groups aren't accountable for breaking natural law.

In fact, if Bob can find a way to argue that *other* people will get a little bit of Tom's money too by supporting the plan, popular support is likely to skyrocket.

This is the first reason many people are persuaded to ignore or break natural law—because it becomes popular.

The second reason is simply that people see governments breaking this natural law all the time, doing all kinds of things that no individual has the right to do.

They witness this so frequently that they just get used to it. Once a society has reached this point, many people are surprised when anyone reminds them that if it isn't right for an individual, it can't be right for government—because all government powers come from individuals joining to delegate their powers.

Regardless of how popular such a policy may be, it is a violation of natural law to delegate to someone else something you don't have—including the authority to steal from someone who has more than you.

Nevertheless, this amazingly obvious truth has been consistently broken by manmade governments. One can argue that this is the single most frequent and worst way in which governments tend to break natural law.

In fact, real freedom is very rare in human history, and it is rare precisely because governments break natural law. If governments all adhered to natural law, freedom and prosperity would be the norm, not a rarity.

Say It Fast Three Times: Pufendorf, Pufendorf, Pufendorf

Here is how Pufendorf taught this principle and how the American founders learned it from his writings:[2]

- No man or woman has the right to do through an alliance with others anything he or she doesn't have the natural right to do alone—and doing so is a harm to all.

- In fact, any person who does this or allows it will owe a debt of fair reparation to the rest of the society.

- No man or woman has the right to *allow* his or her representative(s) to do anything he or she doesn't have the natural right to do alone—and doing so is a harm to all.

- Any person who promotes his or her own advantage or special personal benefit in the name of banding in allegiance for the protection of equal freedom, or joins such an alliance, is at fault of a harm to all.

These obvious—or, as Jefferson said, self-evident—truths are fundamental natural laws. For example, Mary can vote for the candidate promising to repeal the law of gravity, or change the value of π to an even 3, but this is breaking natural law, and the votes won't make it so. Even if a majority of people vote for this, it won't work. Even if human beings unanimously vote for it, it won't happen.

This is why founding father Thomas Jefferson said he trembled for his country because he knew that slavery was breaking natural law and that great pain would come from it.

The same is true if we vote to legalize slavery or to take Tom's money by force and give it to Bob and other people. Unless taking Tom's money is something Mary can do as an individual under natural law—if, for example, Tom robbed Bob and justice requires Tom to compensate Bob for the theft or because some other principle within the bounds of natural law applies—Mary has no authority to vote for or allow a candidate to do it.

Mary can elect an official to do things she can do and to even do them better because the officer of the law has the support of many other people in addition to Mary, but she has no right or authority to have the official do something she has no right to do herself.

That would violate natural law, and there would be unavoidable negative consequences.

Thus, it stands to reason that the officer of the law, and the government itself, never has the authority to do anything an individual can't do under natural law.

This is why founding father Thomas Jefferson said he trembled for his country because he knew that slavery was breaking natural law and that great pain would come from it. Not only was the pain very real for all the slaves and generations of their posterity, but the price of a terrible civil war almost ended the American experiment in freedom.

Similar violations of natural law brought an end to Rome and many other great nations. Even those nations that violated natural law but didn't collapse entirely still faced continual struggles and problems as the natural result of breaking natural law.

CHAPTER 5

THE LAW OF FORCE

HUMANS CAN ONLY MORALLY USE FORCE ON OTHER PEOPLE FOR
SELF-DEFENSE, AND GOVERNMENT CAN ONLY MORALLY USE FORCE
ON PEOPLE FOR THE COLLECTIVE SELF-DEFENSE; ANY OTHER USE
OF GOVERNMENT POWER IS A VIOLATION OF NATURAL LAW.

Frédéric Bastiat popularized this understanding in the nine-
teenth century. Using different words than Locke or Pufendorf,
he taught many of the same principles. Bastiat wrote, "What
then is law? As I have said elsewhere, it is the collective organization
of the individual's right to legitimate self-defense."[1]

There are several important points in this sentence. First, manmade
law is collective organization, meaning that something becomes law
when two or more people get together, establish a rule, and consent
to follow it.

Second, since manmade laws come from individuals working
together, the individual can only delegate such authority as he or she
actually has. This is the same thing Pufendorf and Jefferson taught.

Third, manmade laws are only law when they deal with self-
defense. In other words, Dave and Karen can get together and devise
a plan to help Bill rebuild a fence in his yard that was destroyed by
a storm, but they have no authority to make rebuilding fences, or
funding such rebuilding, into manmade law. They have the individual
authority to go help Bill, voluntarily, and even to invite other people
to join them. But they have no natural authority to force others to help.

In fact, it is part of natural law to voluntarily do as many good
things as possible for people and to invite the help of others, but it
is against natural law to force others to help. Government is force,

pure and simple.[2] And that is why it must have limits because force is dangerous and easily corrupted or abused.

Force Changes Things

For example, if Dave and Karen help Bill and convince ten other neighbors to help him, this is a good neighborhood service project. If they go beyond this and convince the city council to require all neighbors and citizens in town to pay $1,000 each to help rebuild fences, this is a bad law because it violates natural law. Specifically, Karen has no natural right to force John to pay money for somebody else's fence. Nor does Dave or any other person have such a natural right of force.

Both have the right to use force in self-defense but not for other purposes.

If John refuses to help with the service project, the neighbors may think John is greedy or selfish. But something much more drastic occurs as soon as government gets involved.

For example, if the desire to have John pay $1,000 to help rebuild fences is written into law, force will likely be used. The local government might levy fines on John for not submitting his payment, and it can withhold other services for which John pays his taxes. The government may send threatening letters, and eventually it may send officers of the law with guns and warrants.

John, if he continues to refuse to pay his $1,000 for fence rebuilding, as required by the manmade law, will have his property taken (by fines or confiscation), his liberty taken (by arrest), or his life taken (if he tries to defend his property from trespassing officers and their guns). Of course, this is an extreme example, but it is also what happens when the desire to do good things turns into manmade laws that use immoral force in the name of doing good.

Note that in all this, nobody is saying that the neighborhood shouldn't help Bill because as human beings, we really should help those in need. Helping others is part of natural law. But *forcing* someone to help others, when self-defense isn't the issue, is a violation of natural law.

Government is force, and therefore it must be delegated wisely and always limited to its proper role of defense. Karen and Dave probably don't want John to be arrested or shot for not helping rebuild fences, but once the law decides to force people to do good, it turns doing good into a thing backed by force—and at times, eventually, force will be used.

Again, such manmade laws are in conflict with natural law. In short, natural law does not allow any person to use force against another person without negative consequences, unless the force is used in self-defense. And since government is force, it can only be used, according to natural law, to establish and carry out self-defense.

Helping others is part of natural law. But forcing someone to help others, when self-defense isn't the issue, is a violation of natural law.

In other words, there is a different standard when one's defense is at stake. For example, if John walks by Bill's broken fence and does nothing, people may say he is greedy, small-minded, or uncaring, but they won't send officers to fine, arrest, or shoot him.

On the other hand, if John walks by Bill's house and sees Bill being physically assaulted and brutally beaten by a large man and then walks on home without doing anything to protect Bill and even fails to call the authorities, people will accurately describe his actions as neglectful, perhaps cowardly, and certainly wrong. Indeed, under natural law, his inaction is immorally illegal.

This is even more significant if John sees Bill's seven-year-old daughter being beaten or attacked and does nothing. This is because the protection of children and others too weak to defend themselves is a point of self-defense.

We should not kill another person for gain or for almost any other reason, but defending ourselves is an exception. And we should take the same acts of defense for others who cannot defend themselves as we would for ourselves if attacked. These are basics in natural law, fairness, common sense, or what C. S. Lewis called "the Tao."

Lewis wrote, "The Tao, which others may call Natural Law or . . . the First Principles of Practical Reason . . . is not one among a series of possible systems of value. It is the sole source of all value judgments. If it is rejected, all value is rejected. If any value is retained, it is retained."[3]

Another Example

As for manmade law, Dave and Karen can band together to keep people from coming into their yards and assaulting them or their children. They can form a neighborhood watch in which they help each other, or hire an officer, sheriff, or marshal to patrol the area and help protect them. They can establish specific laws detailing what attackers cannot do and how to respond to and punish those who break such laws.

As long as these laws are within the bounds of natural law, such laws will increase the people's access to life, liberty, and the pursuit of happiness. This is what manmade laws that enforce natural law do. Thomas Jefferson said it this way: "No man has a natural right to commit aggression on the equal rights of another, and this is all from which the laws ought to restrain him."

The Limits of Force

To repeat this vital principle: Laws are force because government is force, and force should only be used to protect, not to require people to do nice things. In other words, Dave and Karen have the right to defend themselves from someone attacking their family, and they also have the right to pass laws for such defense—even if those laws require John or anyone else in their society to take action. But they can only pass laws prescribing such actions as they themselves have the right to take.

As long as the actions they take are for self-defense, which includes the defense of family and others, and as long as such laws do not violate natural law, the arrangement is legitimate. This is what Bastiat said when he wrote that manmade law "is the collective organization of the individual's right to legitimate self-defense."[4]

THE LAW OF FORCE

If a decree breaks natural law—if it requires something an individual has no right to do (which is one way to break natural law) or if it is about doing nice things rather than self-defense (which breaks natural law if it authorizes force)—it isn't a legitimate law.

Laws are force because government is force, and force should only be used to protect, not to require people to do nice things.

This remains true no matter how powerful or long-established the government, what government officials say to justify their actions, how many times governments break these laws, or how few people object to such violations.

Again, this can be hard for people to grasp, mainly because we are so used to seeing governments violate these principles, but almost all people naturally understand this when it is explained. It is the simple application of what is fair.

Bastiat wrote: "If each man has the right to defend, even by force, his person, his liberty, and his property, several men have the right to get together, come to an understanding, and organize a collective force to provide regularly for this defense."[5]

Note that the rights of property, liberty, and the pursuit of happiness are direct extensions of the right to life and to defend one's life. As Leo Strauss put it: "The natural right to property is a corollary of the fundamental right of self-preservation. . . . If everyone has the natural right to preserve himself, he necessarily has the right to everything that is necessary for his self-preservation . . ."[6] including property, food, shelter, clothing, savings, liberty from being enslaved, and so on.

Thus, humans really have two great natural rights: the right to self-preservation (which we may establish a government to protect) and the right to pursue happiness (which we achieve best when government protects our rights and leaves us otherwise free).[7]

In short, every manmade law is based on force (because self-defense is the only natural law that allows humans to use forceful government) and therefore must actually provide for the protection of people's inalienable rights. If manmade law is used for any other purpose, it reduces the freedom to pursue happiness, breaking natural law and bringing negative consequences to the nation.

For example, governments may legitimately establish schools, as the American founders did, on the basis that only a widely educated people will be strong and fit to govern themselves and to oversee and maintain effective national security. If governments establish schools for any other reason, they are in violation of natural law.

Likewise, governments may build roads if such roads create the industrial and economic strength necessary for true national security. But if they do it for any other reason besides collective self-defense, they are in violation of natural law, and such programs cause negative consequences.

This principle applies to all laws and government powers, yet modern governments routinely do many things that aren't designed for protection from crime or national security. The consequence is widespread negatives in our modern governments, economies, and societies.

Some may argue that schools or roads (or other government programs) aren't good approaches to create national security, and this is a good debate for society to have. In fact, when government gets involved in such things, it nearly always goes well beyond defense.

As long as the debate is about what provides effective protection of inalienable rights and national security, it is a worthy discussion. But when government does things that have nothing to do with such protections and don't even have protection as their express purpose, it is clearly operating outside natural law.

The Rules

Society may have needs that people should work together to fulfill, but force (and government is always force) can only be legally used if self-defense is required because inalienable rights are at stake.

Bastiat said:

Collective right, then, has its principle, its [very reason for existing], its legitimate basis, in individual right; and the collective force can rationally have no other end, no other function, than that of the individual forces for which it substitutes. . . .

Hence, if anything is self-evident it is this: Law is the organization of the natural right to legitimate self-defense; it is the substitution of collective force for individual forces, to act in the sphere in which they have the right to act, to do what they have the right to do: to guarantee security of person, liberty, and property rights, to cause *justice* to reign over all.

And if there existed a nation constituted on this basis, it seems to me that order would prevail there in fact as well as in theory. It seems to me that this nation would have the simplest, most economical, least burdensome, least disturbing, least officious, most just, and consequently most stable government that can be imagined, whatever its political form may be.[8]

The Law of Plunder

Sadly, Bastiat observed, there are no such nations—not fully. This is true because in all nations, "the law is by no means confined to its proper role. . . . It has put the collective force at the service of those who desire to exploit . . . the person, liberty or property of others; it has converted plunder into a right."[9]

By "plunder," Bastiat meant the stealing of something owned by another.[10] When a person steals from another, it is called theft; but when the government steals from another (meaning that it takes or requires anything for any reason other than legitimate self-defense), it is often considered good policy by those who don't understand natural law.[11]

> *Just fixing this one view of government and natural law in society would change the way we make most governmental decisions and lead to a drastically improved society.*

Just fixing this one view of government and natural law in society would change the way we make most governmental decisions and lead to a drastically improved society. The reason we don't change this, beyond the fact that most people don't understand the first three laws outlined in this book, is because of Bastiat's Law.

Bastiat's Law

People want to be safe, and they want progress. Different people seek success or progress of different kinds in differing ways, but virtually all want some sort of improvement in life.

According to Bastiat, there are two ways to obtain such progress. One is to work for it, overcoming all obstacles and hardships until one's goals are met. The second is to find ways to get one's desires through other people's work.

Most people would rather live off the work of others than engage in the hard work of success on their own. There are two principal ways to obtain what one wants through the work of others. The first is to steal it through crime or invasion, and manmade laws and governments were originally created specifically to protect people from these problems.

The second way to get what one wants from others without working for it is to create societal systems that take money from some and give it to others. Such systems include lower and upper castes, printed money that is used by the masses and inflates while the non-paper assets of the elites appreciate, exclusive educational models that maintain a separation between the elites and the masses, and government systems where a few people govern and dictate to the rest.

Perhaps the most effective way humans have created of living off other people's work and money is exploitive government, where the government programs go far beyond laws of self-defense and create numerous laws that take money from those who work and give it to others who don't.

When the workers are the masses and the recipients are the wealthy, the system is called aristocracy. This is the basis of nearly all class and caste systems through human history. In contrast, when the workers are the masses and the recipients are government officials, the system is called socialism.

Note that there are few, if any, examples in history of any other system besides these two: The masses work, and either the wealthy aristocrats or the powerful government officials take the fruits of their labor.

Also note that in both aristocracy and socialism, those who receive money without work justify their system by promising to help the poor. In aristocracies, this justification is called *noblesse oblige*, which has an ancient pedigree and can be found in many writings through history. In socialistic nations, it is often called *fairness*, *social justice*, *collectivism*, or *redistribution of wealth*.

Of course, natural law supports true fairness and social justice, but frequently governments use these phrases merely to promote a little help to the poor combined with the maintenance of huge power for the elites.

Of course, natural law supports true fairness and social justice, but frequently governments use these phrases merely to promote a little help to the poor combined with the maintenance of huge power for the elites.

In all societies, this arrangement of elites living off the masses is based on taxation and government spending. As mentioned, the elites in both aristocracy and socialism give some help to the underclasses, but they maintain the arrangement in such a way that they stay in power regardless of what happens to the rest of the society.

Such systems still plunder the rightful property of the masses, but they certainly don't call what they do *plunder*. In reality, though, governments steal much more money, life, and liberty from their rightful owners than those we call criminals. As Bastiat put it, "No greater change nor any greater evil could be introduced into society than this: to convert the law into an instrument of plunder."[12]

CHAPTER 6

The Law of Decline
—OR—
What Happens to Nations That Violate Natural Law?

WHEN GOVERNMENTS BREAK NATURAL LAW, THEY BRING THE DECLINE
OF FREEDOM AND THE DECLINE OF PROSPERITY ON THEIR OWN NATION.

The worst way to break natural law is for a government to plunder its people. This is a bold statement, and we will explain the reasons for it in this chapter. To begin, it is worst because it is done using force—and not just any force but the combined force of all people in society, called *government*. And according to natural law, anything taken from the people by the government for any purpose other than protecting inalienable rights (legitimate self-defense) is plunder.[1]

It may be *legal* according to manmade law, but in natural law, it is plunder nonetheless.[2] It is legal, but it is wrong. And it is both immoral and illegal in natural law.

Bastiat said:

> Before going further, I believe I ought to explain what I mean by the word "plunder." I do not use it, as is so often done, in a vague, indeterminate, approximate, or metaphorical sense; I use it in its precise, scientific sense. . . .
>
> When property is transferred without the consent of its owner . . . from the one who possesses it to anyone who has not created it, I say that property rights have been violated, that plunder has occurred. I say that this is precisely what the law

is supposed to oppress always and everywhere. If the law itself commits the act that it is supposed to oppress, I say that this is still plunder and, as far as society is concerned, plunder of an even graver kind.[3]

Plunder is a violation of natural law, whether it is done by a single person, by a band of robbers, or by a government. Since there are negative consequences to breaking natural law, just as there are positive consequences to following natural law, a government that does more than protect inalienable rights brings negative consequences to its nation.

The worst way to break natural law is for a government to plunder its people.

Specifically, when a government breaks natural law, it causes its nation to decline and bring many other negative outcomes. But just what are they? According to Bastiat, nations that violate natural law by doing things that individuals can't do, according to natural law, suffer the following consequences:[4]

- The people won't truly respect the law because they know it is confusing and unfair, benefits some but hurts others, and is widely inconsistent and flawed.

    o   This leads to less respect for the law, the government, and the people who serve as government officials and officers.

    o   It also makes people suspect that most government officials are corrupt in some way.

- The people won't see the law as good or the good as legal; they will think that some good things are illegal while some bad things are legal.

- o Again, this leads to more law breaking and less respect for the government.

- o It also leads people to have less respect for each other.

- o And it leads the society to believe that all people are dishonest in one way or another and to behave accordingly.

- As a result, freedom, opportunity, and equality all decrease over time, and no government programs, promises, or guarantees are able to fix a society where the people have lost some or most of their respect for the law, government, government officials, and even other people.

- The lower classes will distrust the upper classes, and the upper classes will disdain the lower classes.

- All classes will eventually distrust and disdain the government.

- Such a society operates on the basic assumption of mistrust, and any such nation is in decline.

- As a nation declines, its political, educational, and media organizations will operate on the assumption of mistrust, and the economy and culture will further decline.

Obviously, this is not the goal of any successful society. But this is what happens when a nation breaks the principles of natural law. It has happened to many great powers in history, including ancient Israel, Greece, Rome, Spain, the Ottomans, France, Germany, China, Japan, and Britain, among others. And it is clearly happening to the United States and many nations of the free world today.

Thomas Jefferson explained it this way:

[No] man will labour for himself who can make another labour for him. . . . And can the liberties of the nation be thought secure when we have removed their only firm basis, a conviction in the minds of the people that these liberties are the gift of God? That they are not to be violated but with his wrath? Indeed I tremble for my country when I reflect that God is just; that his justice cannot sleep forever.

The law of decline is real. It has been called the law of consequences and also the law of the harvest. In short, we reap what we sow.

The Solution

There is a direct and effective solution to our current decline, which is to immediately "sow" a different set of laws that support natural law. In Bastiat's words, "All we have to do is see whether the law takes from some what belongs to them in order to give it to others to whom it does not belong. We must see whether the law performs, for the profit of one citizen and to the detriment of others, an act which that citizen could not perform himself without being guilty of a crime."[5]

This is the basis of good government—to avoid and protect against violations of the natural law.

> Individuals may combine their right of self-defense to protect themselves and others; this is called manmade law. When individuals create organizations to carry out these laws, these creations are called free governments.

Bastiat's very next sentence tells us how to reverse such national decline: "Repeal such a law without delay. It is not only an iniquity in itself; it is a fertile source of iniquities."[6] In fact, unless such laws are repealed, this kind of law will multiply and infect the whole governmental system.[7] It will cause the end of the nation's world leadership, and eventually the end of its freedoms and prosperity—unless the trend is reversed.

This bears repeating: There is a natural law that is above all manmade laws. Manmade laws are only good to the extent that they conform to natural law. Natural law gives people the right to use force for self-defense, but not to make other people do good things that aren't for self-defense. People should do many good things, but force may only be used, according to natural law, in self-defense.

Individuals may combine their right of self-defense to protect themselves and others; this is called manmade law. When individuals create organizations to carry out these laws, these creations are called free governments. According to natural law, a manmade government has the right to do only what an individual has the natural authority to do.

Manmade laws and governments must follow natural law, or negative consequences will inevitably follow. When a society is experiencing widespread negative trends (or decline), it can fix nearly all of them by repealing all laws that violate natural law or adding such laws as are needed to bring the society in line with natural law.

Ours is such a society today, and the law of delegation is real. Our governments today do many things beyond their proper role of protecting inalienable rights, and until this is changed we will not see the problems in our politics and society fixed. Elections will come and go, parties will win and lose, and yet the problems will continue—until we lose nearly all our freedoms or until we get our laws and government in line with natural law.

It is time for modern society to understand natural law and to make this change. But time is running out. . . .

THE PROPER ROLE OF GOVERNMENT

"**A**re you there?" he asked.

"Yes, good. That's a much better connection," I said. "Where are you?"

"I'm at an event in Columbus, Ohio, and right now, I'm in my hotel room. I've got a couple of hours before my next speech and no other meetings until this evening, so let's discuss roads and schools like we planned."

"Great," I carried the cell phone out of my room and out the back door so I could be in the sun while we talked. "This really is the crux of natural law because it is where this whole thing gets practical."

"Before we start," he said, "I just want to be sure we're in agreement on one thing." Then his voice turned deep and husky as he repeated, "Pufendorf, Pufendorf, Pufendorf."

I chuckled as I walked up the driveway past the grove of green quaking aspens and tall pine trees. "Did you use that in your speech this morning?" I asked.

"Absolutely! It was my first point, my second point, and also my third point," he joked.

"I bet that brought a standing ovation," I said lightly. I sat down on a big piece of cedar at the edge of the large woodpile.

"It's just such a funny name," he said, "and when I first heard it, I thought it must be made up, not a real name."

"So you say it repeatedly in a deep voice?" I asked.

"Seemed like a good idea at the time."

"I'll keep that in mind."

"Okay, seriously," he said, "I've been thinking more about your chapter on the law of delegation. Pufendorf and Bastiat are really firm that government can't legitimately do anything beyond collective self-defense, but the founders wrote a bunch of things into the Constitution that aren't national defense—like the post office, weights and measures, and building roads. Did they disagree with Pufendorf and Locke, or did they just fudge their principles when it felt like some things were really needed?"

He kept talking, answering his own question. "You know what I think? I think they did what most politicians do—they taught principles when they were speaking or campaigning, but then when they were in office, they just did what seemed needful even if it went against the principles."

He paused, and I spoke. "Actually, I think they saw all those things as national security issues. I mean, think about it. In their day, roads were a military necessity, almost an extension of forts and garrisons. Where there were no roads, they lost most of their skirmishes in the French and Indian War and the Revolutionary War, and they won when they could get their troops where they were needed. And remember, the Constitution was written in 1787, just two years after the end of the Revolutionary War."

"That's right," he said. "And nations that didn't closely watch the weights and measures in those days saw their currencies counterfeited, not just by cheaters but also by enemy nations. And a government postal service was the only way to protect military communications. I get that. So in their day, these things were an extension of self-defense, while in our time, they aren't."

"True, assuming that we remain at the same level of technology and don't slide back to more limited communications and transportation," I replied. "And I think you can make the case that a good military strategy would keep those things as a Plan B, just in case."

"Schools and health care are more difficult," he said.

I took off my hat so the fall sun would hit me full in the face. Then I responded, "They are. But the Constitution left them both to the states, not the federal government. Still, the first law passed by the new Congress after the Constitution was ratified required the states to have an educational system."

"Actually, I thought that law, the Northwest Ordinance, just required any new territory that wanted to become a state to have a good education system, right?" he asked.

"You're right," I said. "I stand corrected. They didn't force the existing states to open schools, but the states did anyway, and any new state had to do the same. So, in effect, while the Constitution didn't directly build schools, the states did. The question is do government schools violate the law of delegation?"

In their day, roads were a military necessity, almost an extension of forts and garrisons. Where there were no roads, they lost most of their skirmishes in the French and Indian War and the Revolutionary War, and they won when they could get their troops where they were needed.

"Meaning," he countered, "do they do something as a group and through government force that no individual has the right to do through force on his own?"

"Exactly."

"Well," he said, "are government schools built for self-defense, either from crime or foreign aggression? The question really is that simple."

"Yes, but I think we have to ask two different questions. First, why do we build and fund government schools today? And second, did the founders build them for reasons of national defense? These are really different things."

"Okay, I can see that. Let's start with the founding because it's pretty clear to me that our reasons for modern government schools have gone way beyond defense and national security. What about the founders? Did they build state schools for reasons of defense?"

"I think they did," I said. "I used to totally disagree with this. When I first read *The Law* by Bastiat many years ago, I was immediately convinced that all government schools violated natural law. But when I actually read the writings of the founders, I realized that they saw schools as the first line of self-defense and national security. In fact, Jefferson's writings are just full of this idea. He thought that without state schools available for every child in the country, the new nation would have no chance of remaining free and independent from the powers of Europe."

"Really?"

"George Washington even wanted the *federal* government to get involved in education, especially at the collegiate level, to create a national university that would train leaders at a higher level than the European universities. His reason was to help keep America strong and free from European aggression. This never fully happened, but it eventually resulted in the military academies like West Point and the Naval Academy. For many of the founders, education and national security were inseparably linked."

> *When I actually read the writings of the founders, I realized that they saw schools as the first line of self-defense and national security.*

"I understand the military academies, but I could argue all day against the wisdom of the rest of that," he said. "Still, let's just say for the sake of argument that the founders were right. Even so, it's a very slippery slope, don't you think?"

I laughed. "Absolutely. I mean, clearly the last two hundred years have proven that when government gets involved in anything beyond stopping criminals and invasions, it pretty much always goes too far. That's just the way it happens, as Pufendorf, Jefferson, and Bastiat predicted. So yes, it was a slippery slope. The founders wanted the states to encourage good schools and offer them where they were needed in order to maintain long-term national security, but over two hundred years later the consequence has been massive government intrusion in education—and the biggest problem is intervention from Washington, not from the states.

"Where the founders wanted all schools run privately or by local school boards made up of the parents in the town or county, we now have a bureaucratic mess run mostly from Washington. And many parents feel as helpless to change things as our students. I don't see anything in the founders' writings that indicates they would like the current system—not at all."

"It's even worse than that," he said. Then he took a deep breath. "Let's look at this from another angle to show what I mean. What percentage of government programs in the United States, Canada, or Europe do you think is spent on protecting inalienable rights from crime and invasion, and what percentage has nothing to do with protections at all?

"Let's just pretend that education is for long-term defense, though I think it really isn't anymore, if it ever was," he continued. "But even if we keep all education, all of the military (even though it has gone way past its purpose of defense and gotten involved all around the world) and keep all the teachers, police officers, courts, fire fighters, and every other government program that has any claim at all to protecting our rights, does all of that account for even half of the government's annual expenses?"

"I see where you're going," I said, "and you're right. The federal government spends about 3 percent on education, 20 percent on defense and security, and 7 percent on benefits for government retirees and veterans. Together, those add up to 30 percent. But 61 percent is spent on various safety nets and on interest on the debt. And by the way, the interest is going up fast."

"That's my point," he said. "Whether the law of delegation applies to education or not, it only accounts for 3 percent of our federal spending, although it costs the states more. But we've got 61 percent that is mostly violating natural law because no individual has the right to force his neighbors to pay for those things. I think the solution is to use the 3 percent all at the local level and to set up an effective voucher system that gives real choice to parents. These two simple changes would give freedom a true chance, and freedom can actually fix education."

"Get education off the conveyor belt!" I agreed.

"Exactly," he said. "Even if we conceded every point about education and self-defense—which I don't, but just for the sake of argument, let's assume I do—we could fix education simply by handling the money locally and giving parents real choice."

"I agree," I said. "And we should also help more teachers and parents realize what really works in education, which is to find effective ways to help each student become actively involved in leading his or her own education."

"You wrote about how to do that in your book *A Thomas Jefferson Education*," he said, "but I have a bigger point. We can debate the 3 percent—and I think we should at some point because, as Bastiat said, the only way to save a nation that is in the clutches of plundering government is to repeal any manmade law or policy that violates natural law—but the place to start is with the 61 percent."

I put my hat back on and turned so the other side of my face would get the sun. "And we should also note that in almost every summary of the budget, there is a big chunk of our spending, around 9 percent, that is always listed as 'other.' If we want to be free, we really need to give serious thought to that word *other* and what's hiding behind it."

He laughed at the absurdity of it all.

"What's funny?" I asked.

"The whole thing." He went on in a mix of bemusement and frustration. "It's not really funny at all, but then it's so big that it's just . . ." He strained to find the right word.

"Amazing?" I suggested.

He agreed. "It really is. It's just plain amazing—and not in a good way."

"Bastiat was right," I acknowledged. "When we start allowing one or a few laws that go beyond the limits of natural law, the whole thing snowballs, and pretty soon, the entire society has become committed to expanding complex and hurtful policies."

"He was also right about the solution," he firmly declared. "If we start repealing or changing one or a few such laws, people will feel more freedom and want to keep going in the right direction. God's natural laws really are that powerful."

I watched the leaves quake on the aspens. "It's such a beautiful world we live in," I said quietly. "So much good in it, and so many good people."

He laughed. "You know, that's one of those comments that might seem to have nothing to do with the conversation—to anyone who didn't know you. But I know what you mean. We're going to win this thing. I know we are. Natural law is the real answer, not bigger and bigger government."

"I think we're done for now, don't you?" I asked.

"Yes. But this conversation isn't even close to finished. We haven't even started working through every specific detail. We've got to hold everything, every single government policy, up to the standard of natural law and see which laws should stay and which must be changed."

"Absolutely. I'll get started tonight," I said. "Right now, I need to chop some wood with Ammon. We're getting our woodpile ready for winter; then I'm reading *Trumpet of the Swan* to the kids this evening. When do you want to talk next?"

"I want to focus on this event here in Ohio for the next two days," he said. "I'll call you Monday, or you call me if you stay up all night writing again, okay?"

CHAPTER 7

THE LAW OF POWER

IT IS THE NATURE OF POWER TO TRY TO CENTRALIZE,
AND ONCE IT IS CENTRALIZED TO ATTEMPT TO EXPAND ITS CONTROL.

The comedian Rita Rudner once said, "I was going to have cosmetic surgery until I noticed that the doctor's office was full of portraits by Picasso."

Nobody wants Picasso as their cosmetic surgeon. His cubist style of painting breaks everything—faces, bodies, larger scenes—into pieces and rearranges them in misshapen ways. Instead of looking like nature, his works are beyond abstract. They show reality but distorted and warped, still recognizable but clearly deformed.

In truth, such twisted portrayals are often more truthful than the real thing. Picasso aimed to show the ugly that sometimes hides in well-designed facades that are meant to make good look bad and bad look good. Government has a long history of using such facades to hide what it is really doing.

Picasso's style is a good template for political analysis because it emphasizes the truth behind the outward show or public image portrayed by too many governments through history. By breaking up the façade and showing what is behind the curtain, citizens spread freedom because they are able to see what is real and what isn't.

> *People who wield power influence all of us, whether the power is used openly or in concealed ways. As a result, understanding power is vital to maintaining freedom.*

In a profound nineteenth-century essay that taught this same theme, Frédéric Bastiat wrote that life is made up to two things:

(1) what is seen, or the façades society presents, and (2) what is not seen, meaning the truth of hidden designs and actions.[1]

Applying such Picasso-like thinking, it is clear that few things are as important to understand as the law of power. People who wield power influence all of us, whether the power is used openly or in concealed ways. As a result, understanding power is vital to maintaining freedom.

In all of this, the solution to the law of power is the law of the gaps. Let's consider both of these laws and how they work together.

The Power Principle

It is the nature of all power to centralize into the hands of one person, place, institution, or entity and then, once it is fully controlled by one person or thing, to expand its domination as far and wide as possible. Power doesn't naturally seek to limit itself. It seeks to dominate. This is true in the astronomical, physical, and biological realms, and it is true in human societies, relationships, and political arrangements. It is true within nations and in international relations.

Energy, as opposed to power, often naturally dissipates because it is constantly flowing and reorganizing. But power stops the natural entropy of energy, seeking always to control.

Through most of humankind's history, this principle has manifested in the creation of monarchical societies, whether in small tribes dominated by chiefs or kings or in larger societies with emperors, caesars, tsars, dictators, prime ministers, presidents, or chairmen. And this principle has lasted through human history, from the times of Julius Caesar and Genghis Khan to the era of Josef Stalin and Chairman Mao.

At times, a second arrangement has prevailed, centralizing power in a group of aristocratic families or oligarchs. Through history, aristocracies and monarchies have continually competed for dominance.

This is the law of power: it attempts to centralize and dominate and then to expand its dominance as widely as possible. As a result, societies with widespread freedom and opportunity for all people have been very rare. And where such uncommon free societies have arisen, freedom has been found *in the gaps*. This means that widespread liberty and economic opportunity are nearly always found in the areas that those in power have failed to closely dominate.

Freedom in the Gaps

For example, in the ancient world, the gaps existed in the small tribal areas that were far from the centers of human empire. As long as such tribes remained "off the radar" of the empires, city-states, and conquerors jockeying for power, they were places of relative peace, freedom, and economic opportunity. The big powers did not focus on controlling such outlying areas, and to the extent that they were ignored, they frequently remained free.

In medieval times, nearly all towns and villages were under the expanding control of the various kingdoms and feudal fiefdoms, and much of the economy was regulated by guilds. The gaps were found in the bands of traveling merchants who had their own small armies and traveled from kingdom to kingdom carrying goods, spices, silks, and assorted other merchandise.

Each small kingdom benefitted from the services of the merchants, and to a large extent, the members of these traveling caravans experienced relative freedom and economic opportunity outside the controlling force of kings, aristocrats, governing clergy, guild boards, and their agents. The Crusades were part of this trend and provided opportunity for the non-heir children of the European aristocracies— as well as ordinary people—to distinguish themselves by their actions and initiative rather than being limited by inherited station.

In the age of exploration and the American founding eras, the gaps were found on the frontier. Even as late as the American Civil War, people could find significant freedom and economic opportunity by pioneering the unsettled and largely unregulated lands in the North American West—from the Canadian plains and Rocky Mountains all the way south into central Mexico. Similar expansion took fortune hunters to the Latin Americas, Africa, the Pacific Islands, and Asian arenas, as well as the Indian subcontinent.

Anglo-American Gaps

The American founding generation understood this concept of centralizing and expanding power, as well as the idea that freedom and opportunity are found in the gaps where no elites or aristocrats have yet expanded their power. The framers were deeply aware of the battle for dominance between the English monarchy and the Parliament, and they realized that historically, the gaps in English freedom had always existed in the places where neither of these powers was entirely dominant.

Specifically, Virginia, Massachusetts, and New York were royal colonies that had a governor who reported directly to the king. This meant that nothing the Parliament of England did had direct power over them. In contrast, colonies like Pennsylvania, Maryland, and Rhode Island were not royal colonies, and the English Parliament acted as if it always had direct power to regulate their affairs.

There was a significant and noticeable difference between the royal and nonroyal colonies, and the colonists were especially sensitive to it because through English history, Ireland had been dominated by the English Parliament, while Scotland had much more freedom and its own parliament elected by the Scottish people.

> *The American founding generation understood this concept of centralizing and expanding power, as well as the idea that freedom and opportunity are found in the gaps where no elites or aristocrats have yet expanded their power.*

Both Ireland and Scotland were considered under the king, but the Scots has their own elected leaders, while the Irish had little protection against anything the English Parliament decided to inflict on them. Thus, for nearly a thousand years, the Irish were subject to exorbitant taxes, English troops patrolling their cities and communities, and English soldiers marching into yards and homes and hauling their youth away to serve in the military—without parental permission and despite the protests of the people.

By contrast, the Scots faced fewer of these injustices.

Thus, the Scottish people lived in the gaps (where jurisdiction over the people was disputed between the king and the Scottish Parliament with little or no control from the English Parliament), while the Irish people were clearly under the control of London. The American framers were aware of this and understood that freedom resides in the gaps, in places where power is in dispute and not fully dominant.

Likewise, in the American royal colonies like Virginia, Massachusetts, and New York, the power of the king kept the English Parliament from dominating, and the locals ran their own parliaments for many decades. All such parliaments ultimately reported to the king or his governor, but they allowed a great level of self-government that created a culture and citizenry closely involved in politics.

In this situation, where the English Parliament had no authority and the governing power was split between the king, governor, and local parliament, the gap in dominance allowed significant freedom. These three colonies, operating in the gaps where no one institution of government fully dominated, created most of the leadership for the American Revolution and founding.

In fact, the revolution itself was spurred precisely when the English Parliament closed the gap and began exerting influence on Massachusetts through a tax on tea. With the history of Scotland versus Ireland clearly in their minds, the people of Boston and the surrounding countryside considered this change unbearable.

Today, we must not forget the law of power. Government power is centralizing, and right now it's drastically expanding. Only a people who always remember this can keep an eye on it and protect their freedoms.

CHAPTER 8

THE LAW OF GAPS

FREEDOM IS FOUND IN THE GAPS
WHERE GOVERNMENTS COMPETE FOR POWER.

The great classical thinker Montesquieu wrote, "When the legislative and executive powers are united in the same person, or in the same body of magistrates, there can be no liberty. . . . Again, there is no liberty, if the judiciary power be not separated from the legislative and executive."

As a result of understanding the history of the law of gaps, when the framers wrote the US Constitution, they did so with the specific design of creating lasting gaps where freedom could flourish. They knew that it is the nature of power to try to centralize and dominate and then to expand its dominance far and wide, so they created a multiheaded government with separated powers that would continually fight each other and keep any one entity from getting full power.

The Ten Branches of Government

In fact, though there were four major branches of government written into the Constitution (legislative in Article I of the Constitution, executive

> *"There is no liberty, if the judiciary power be not separated from the legislative and executive."*
> — *Montesquieu*

in Article II, judicial in Article III, and the states in Article IV), the system actually established ten branches of government. The ten competing heads of this government were the following:

1. The executive branch (presidency), which would represent the nation mainly in preserving its national security

2. The spending branch (House), which would see national needs and implement national solutions

3. The aristocratic branch (Senate), which would keep most of the ambitious leaders in one place where they could be closely watched by all and which would also naturally tend to keep the spending branch of government in check

4. The judicial branch (Supreme Court), which would represent the Constitution and keep the other branches from exceeding their written powers

5. The governing branch (states), which were given authority to oversee and implement most government actions across the nation

6. The participative branch (local governments), which would keep the people involved and train them to participate in governance and maintain their freedoms

7. The checking branch (juries), which would be able to keep government in line if it unjustly attacked the regular people

8. The second backup checking branch (grand juries), which would keep the government in line even if the regular jury system began to fail

9. The federalizing branch (Electoral College), which would ensure that the chief executive would represent all the states rather than just a few of the most populated states

10. The overseer branch (voters), who would closely watch the entire system and keep it in line through regular elections and ongoing participation between elections

This is another place where it would be easy to turn off, ignore these details, and leave the future of freedom to the experts. But unless you and I study this, we'll lose our freedoms. The current decline will continue.

This system was designed so that when any one government entity or official tried to exert too much power, the others would naturally take action to put it back in its place.

Such a model kept many gaps in place through American history, which created great freedom and economic opportunity and helped the United States become the freest and most powerful nation in the world.

Under this system, by 1945, with just 6 percent of the world's population, the United States was creating more than half of the world's goods and services—not by government planning, but mostly through voluntary free enterprise. The law of power was harnessed to allow the law of gaps to work.

Unfortunately, by that same year, changes to the system were already in place that would allow power to centralize and close the gaps that had brought such widespread American success.[1]

Freedom's Success Formula

To summarize, the American freedom success formula was to create a government that was neither monarchy nor aristocracy and not simply oligarchy, democracy, or republic but in fact a type of democratic republic that combined elements from all these historical forms of government.

The American freedom success formula was to create a government that was neither monarchy nor aristocracy and not simply oligarchy, democracy, or republic but in fact a type of democratic republic that combined elements from all these historical forms of government.

In a monarchy, all power centralizes in the king and then spreads to dominate all parts of society, while in an aristocracy, all power centralizes in the aristocratic families or institutions and then swells until it controls the entire nation.

Likewise, in most democracies through history, the power of the people has eventually centered in one group of people and then spread to remove the freedom of the rest. Similarly, in the ancient and medieval republics, the power centralized into either the kingly or the parliamentary branch and then expanded its control over everyone.

All the ancient Greek federations, medieval European republics, and modern Germanic and Italian confederations followed this same pattern—as discussed by James Madison in *Federalist* 18, 19, and 20—with power centralizing in one or another branch of government and then broadening to take control of the whole society. Over and over, freedom was lost following this pattern.

The American framers understood this pattern, and so they wrote the Constitution with all ten branches of government listed above in mind.

They knew that all ten branches would attempt to centralize power, and they hoped that the other nine branches would work together to keep any one branch from becoming dominant. As this battle between the ten branches raged over the decades, they knew the gaps where no one branch controlled everything would keep the nation generally free. In the process, the ten branches would cooperate as needed to thwart any great national security threats but continually compete with each other on every other issue.

The result, they hoped, would be more gaps, more freedom, and lasting economic opportunity for all.

The Plan in Action

The history of the United States has proven the effectiveness, and also the flaws, of this model. Through American history, some of the ten branches have tried to take full power, but in most cases, they were thwarted by one or more of the other nine branches.

Through American history, some of the ten branches have tried to take full power, but in most cases, they were thwarted by one or more of the other nine branches.

For example, from 1792 to 1800, the great battle was the attempt of the House to dominate American politics, but this was refuted by the strength of the federal system and especially the strong executive policies of Alexander Hamilton.

In the Jeffersonian era from 1800 to 1824, the Marshall Court attempted to exert dominance over all branches of government, but the Jeffersonian presidents (Jefferson, Madison, and Monroe) mostly checked the court's expansion of power.

Between 1824 and 1856, the power of local governments became increasingly dominant, and people of minority races, religions, gender, and views were frequently deprived of freedoms and opportunities—often through the use of violence. The attacks on freedom frequently went too far, usually because of inaction from state governments. During this period, the judiciary also failed by allowing far too many violations of the inalienable rights of various citizens, culminating in the Jim Crow laws.

Such abuses should have been righted sooner but were eventually dealt with by the federalizing branch of government (the Electoral College) as the growing number of Western states increased their influence. The frontier to the West allowed people to travel to the unincorporated wilderness and find freedom and economic opportunities in the gaps outside the Eastern states.

From 1856 to 1896, the power of the states, which attempted to create provincial dominance in both the North and the South, was tempered by the combined powers of the spending, executive, and aristocratic branches in Washington. None of this was ideal, but the Civil War era and its aftermath would almost certainly have been much worse if power had fully centralized in any one collection of states or any one branch of government. For example, without the actions of the House and Senate, the executive power of the carpetbagger era might well have reduced the power of the South forever.

Of course, when we attempt to speculate about what would have happened if history had gone differently, we are always guessing, but the history of the world makes it clear that major civil war has nearly always led to the end of serious national cooperation. America's post–Civil War healing, though it took a long time, is a surprising exception in world history, and one important reason is the stabilizing reality of having ten—rather than one—powerful heads (branches) of the government.

The progressive era from 1896 to 1945 was dominated by an aristocratic Senate but kept at least partially in check by the combined state governments.

Toward the end of this period of senatorial power, and presaging the era of executive dominance to come, President Franklin Delano Roosevelt's attempt to stack the Supreme Court by expanding its size and filling the new spots with judges who supported his policies was effectively opposed by the legislative branch and by the court itself. This was one of the most openly obvious attempts in US history to centralize power into one institution of government.

The post-1945 era became an age of executive expansion, as the power of government has continually centralized into the executive branch of government. During this period, the number of national executive branch departments, agencies, and programs has drastically grown. Sadly, though the courts and Congress have slowed this spread of power over time, they have done nothing to effectively stop this trend.

In short, the whole experiment with ten branches of government has been a success and also a failure. It certainly slowed the centralizing of power to one government entity, and it also reduced the spread of executive and judicial power over the rest of the nation more than in any other society in history. But the law of power is still strongly at work.

The Coming Challenge

Power has centralized in Washington, starting in 1803 and increasing during the Civil War, progressive era, Great Depression, World War II, and especially the international era since 1945. As it has centralized, it has also expanded.

Today this centralizing trend is on the verge of destroying the American system of separate branches of government, checks and balances, and protection of inalienable rights that created unprecedented levels of freedom and widespread economic opportunity known as the American Dream.

Freedom is still, as always, found in the gaps, but as Washington gains more power over our lives, there are fewer and fewer areas of opportunity that aren't closely regulated and dominated by government. Unless this is reversed, and soon, the American experiment in freedom is in certain decline and serious jeopardy.

CHAPTER 9

THE LAW OF THE VITAL FEW

THROUGH HISTORY, REAL FREEDOM ULTIMATELY DEPENDS ON THE
LEADERSHIP OF A FEW ORDINARY PEOPLE
WHO DO EXTRAORDINARY THINGS.

The modern gaps are found mostly in the arena of entrepreneurship. Indeed, the best place to find gaps where freedom and opportunity flourish is in situations where initiative and risk bring success—rather than economic sectors that emphasize experts and institutions. There are many such prospects, though their frequency is in decline in the current system.

As author Phil Cooke put it, "Success happens in spite of bad statistics, a terrible economy, and horrendous odds."[1] The great writer Jack London said succinctly, "You can't wait for inspiration. You have to go after it with a club."[2]

What is needed is a new generation of American founders, not just in the United States but also in Canada, Europe, and all nations of the free world that are undergoing a similar centralizing and expanding of government power—and the resulting decline of freedom and prosperity.

Despite the welcome contributions of great leaders, entrepreneurs, and innovators, the governmental system has a huge impact on freedom and opportunity. In order to maintain a society where freedom and economic prosperity are the norm, our generation needs more people who exert leadership to keep the government free.

The law of power is a natural law, as is the law of the gaps. And over time, power has increasingly centralized in Washington, the executive branch, and the judiciary. As mentioned, this dangerous trend simply must be addressed and reversed, or America will drastically decline and levels of freedom and opportunity will continue to decrease.

What is needed is a new generation of American founders, not just in the United States but also in Canada, Europe, and all nations of the free world that are undergoing a similar centralizing and expanding of government power—and the resulting decline of freedom and prosperity.

Power and Spoils

Einstein's advice is especially applicable to our day: "Out of clutter, find simplicity. From discord, find harmony. In the middle of difficulty, lies opportunity."[3]

Since freedom is found in the gaps, the simple solution is for one or more of the other nine branches of government to exert effective opposition to the centralization of executive national power.

This brings us to a corollary of the law of power, which is that one major reason power centralizes is that increased power in one branch offers amplified spoils to those who ally with it. Specifically, in the case of the United States, the Senate, House, and Supreme Court have gained significant benefits by allowing power to centralize in the national executive.

As the relative importance of Washington and the White House have grown, the clout, benefits, salaries, and ability to spend the nation's money have drastically increased for the Senate and House, and by extension, the courts.

Indeed, since the unfortunate adoption of the Seventeenth Amendment and direct election of US Senators by popular vote, none of the federal branches are directly benefitted by seeing power decentralize away from Washington and back to the states, locales, juries, the private sector, or the people.

Likewise, the courts have taken direct action to penalize members of juries and grand juries who use these powers to check the government, and over the decades, these two branches have ceased to be effective in stopping the centralization of power to the White House, Pentagon, Treasury and State Departments, and so on.

Congress and the courts have combined to make the state and local branches of government dependent on federal funding, and as a result, state or local governments that stand up to federal mandates are infrequent and usually unsuccessful in court.

Thus, with the executive branch intent on centralizing its power, the courts and two branches of Congress gaining direct spoils from this centralization, and the increasing impotence of the state, local, jury, and grand jury branches in checking the national executive, only two branches are left that have any chance of fixing our national decline.

Gap Solutions

Note that in most nations with fewer than ten branches of government, this dominance of the national executive is already complete, and unless the two remaining independent branches of American governance take effective action in the next few years, the law of power will continue to close the gaps of freedom and free enterprise.

The two branches that still have a significant nonexecutive say in American leadership are the Electoral College and the American voters—both of which boil down to two things: (1) elections and (2) ongoing, daily participation in government by the citizens.

Indeed, the power of American government now only has two great centers: the federal government on one side (with the executive in charge and strongly supported by the courts and the Senate) and the American voters and citizens on the other.

This is the epicenter and the crux of the battle, and the future of America will come down to how our citizenry utilizes its significant power.

Indeed, it is in this very reality that the brilliance of the American founding fathers is most manifest. It also pinpoints their greatest weakness. Specifically, as badly as America has gone off track in recent decades, the Constitution still gives the people the final say. We may or may not use it wisely, we may rise up and use our power or simply ignore it, or we may follow the lead of the elite media. But it is still up to us.

Critics of the founders might argue that freedom is far too important to leave in the hands of the masses, but in history, no other group has been more effective in protecting the freedom of the people than the masses themselves.

So what can we do? Put simply, more power must be returned to local areas. As Jefferson said, the key to maintaining freedom is to "divide and subdivide" government power. If local governments have more power, more citizens will be involved in everyday government.

If we vote for a further centralization of power to the national executive (either out of ignorance or because we are swayed by the media), we will get a nation dominated by Washington's power and a corresponding decline of freedom and widespread prosperity. If, in contrast, we as a people vote for a future of freedom and greater economic opportunity, that is what we will get.

The founders, reaching into our day with their decisions two centuries past, have put the most important American decision ultimately in our hands, and our choices will determine the future.

The Choice

This brings us to three vital choices this generation will make, all of which will be extraordinarily impactful on the world we will pass on to our children and grandchildren. Let's consider these choices in reverse order, with the most important choice last.

Note that candidates from both major parties, and the presidents we have actually elected from both parties for the last three decades, have grown the national executive.

The third most important choice of our generation is who we elect as president every four years (or as the leading party and therefore the prime minister in parliamentary nations). Such elections set the tone of the national executive and whether the administration emphasizes fast or slow growth of Washington's power.

Note that candidates from both major parties, and the presidents we have actually elected from both parties for the last three decades, have grown the national executive—centralizing power to Washington and the White House, and then spreading this power throughout the nation and around the globe.

Neither party has recently produced a president who fought the law of power in order to promote the law of gaps.

With that said, some candidates and presidents focus on fast growth of the national executive and others on slower growth, and while both are bad for the future of freedom and prosperity, faster growth is much worse than slower expansion of Washington's power.

> *The current political party system keeps the middle class from uniting and truly fixing major national problems.*

Citizens stand up for freedom when they think independently, refusing to be swayed by the agendas or propaganda of media organizations or political parties. For example, the opposite of the law of gaps is that freedom can be reduced when big voting blocs are divided. Specifically, if the ultra-elite can divide the hard-working middle class so that half of them are Democrats and the other half Republicans, the elites will win most elections. If the middle class voted in unison against elite schemes and proposals, we could fix Washington quickly.

As it stands, when one party wins an election by a large majority, the ultra-elite class swings its support behind the other party to balance power. This happens repeatedly, with power and support swinging back and forth from one party to the other. As a result, big promises are made. But government spending seldom gets cut, and debts and deficits climb regardless of who is in office. The current political party system keeps the middle class from uniting and truly fixing major national problems.

Second Choice

The second most important choice in our generation is our vote for our representatives in the House (or those with the powers of the purse in parliamentary nations). If we don't limit government spending, we can't limit government.

As the spending branch of government, the House has the most ability to slow the growth of the national executive. In fact, though it has shown little will to use its power, the House is the one remaining branch of the federal government most likely to stop the centralization of power to the executive.

If there is any chance of reversing our modern loss of freedom (which will occur when power is fully centralized to the national executive), it is in the House. The voters have the power every two years to entirely change the House, to elect those who will truly change things—or not.

It is in this power that America has a chance, and if we don't win this battle, we won't win at all. Freedom will be lost, and the founding fathers' experiment in freedom will be over. We are currently on track for this result of lost freedom, and it is no exaggeration to say that the House is our last (political) chance to save the republic.

Top Choice

This brings us to the most important choice we can make to save our nations, which is to take personal action that preserves freedom. There are two major ways to do this. One is to have an ongoing influence on what government is doing, especially by watching the House and getting deeply involved in what our representatives do day in and day out. We literally need a number of citizens who get to know their representatives and stay actively involved in watching and influencing their choices.

This means involvement between elections, which is much more important than mere voting.

Every citizen has the ability to get involved at this level.

The second thing the average citizen can do is to get enthusiastically involved in creating and spreading entrepreneurship and mini-factories.[4] Mini-factories are organizations—business or nonprofit—that engage people in important undertakings that directly benefit society.

Such enterprises may include starting an organization, building a network marketing business, establishing and running a local school or charity, or actively supporting one that is already in place. The key is to build community.

In every community there are entities that need volunteers and donors, and there are needs for help in hospitals, churches, youth organizations, libraries, scouts, sporting leagues, and other groups where your service and support can make a huge difference.

In declining nations, people work to make a living and otherwise mostly stay home, leaving others to handle the needs of the community. But this has the effect of depriving society of their talents, abilities, and passion and only adds to the decline and loss of freedom.

In declining nations, people work to make a living and otherwise mostly stay home, leaving others to handle the needs of the community. But this has the effect of depriving society of their talents, abilities, and passion and only adds to the decline and loss of freedom.

The Law of the Vital Few

We desperately need a certain type of citizen in our modern society, the kind of person who, like the American founding generations, gets out and gets actively involved in addressing the needs of our communities.

This is the true hope of our free nations: people who take initiative on their own without government, spreading philanthropy, building businesses, volunteering and serving, looking around to see what is needed, and organizing people to improve our neighborhoods and towns.

This is the foundation and secret of every free culture, and it is based on regular people who are innovators and initiators—people who take action to improve society without waiting for government.

We need to build things, make things happen, spread opportunity and service, expand entrepreneurship in our communities, and inspire people to live up to their potential instead of settling for the mediocrity that is the norm in declining nations.

The law of power says that control is always trying to centralize and expand, but every time an individual takes independent action, starts something, volunteers, leads, builds the community, or inspires initiative, power is decentralized and freedom spreads. Personal action matters, and natural law promises increased energy and influence to those whose innovation, hard work, and tenacity create community, prosperity, and leadership in places far from the centers of power.

Indeed, ultimately the law of gaps supersedes the law of power, just as the law of lift overcomes the law of gravity because natural law rewards initiative, innovation, hard work, and tenacity. Success breeds success, leadership breeds leadership, and freedom breeds freedom.

This is a law of nature, and the future of freedom depends on the few—the entrepreneurial few—who take the risk of aiming for greatness and refusing to settle for societal norms of mediocrity.

In this way, according to natural law, the actions of a few change the reality for everyone. This is the law of the vital few,[5] and it is exemplified by ordinary people who do extraordinary things without waiting for the direction or permission of officials or governments.

The American founding generation was led by just such individuals, and a new crop of such leaders is desperately needed again in our day.

It is a natural law that true leadership more frequently arises from average citizens, in contrast to the elite classes that too often tend to hold back real progress. But the actual number of such leaders is few. It is likely that if you are reading this book, you are capable of being one of these leaders. And now is the time to take action.

CHAPTER 10

THE LAW OF LIBERTY

WHEN FREEDOM IS REDUCED FOR SOME, IT IS REDUCED FOR ALL.

American founding father James Otis said in 1764, "The Parliament cannot make two and two, five. . . . Should an act of Parliament be against any of his [the Creator's] natural laws, their declaration would be contrary to eternal truth, equity, and justice, and consequently void."[1]

One of the great natural laws we most need to understand today is the law of liberty, which says that freedom is truly indivisible because taking it from some ultimately reduces the freedom of everyone. This natural law is sometimes ignored for the simple reason that it isn't always obvious in the short term, just as the reality that the earth is round isn't always clearly evident to the naked eye.

Because this law isn't apparent unless a person understands it, generations of human beings have reduced their own freedoms because

> *In the same way that government often gets away with spending on things that break natural laws because the citizens think it is spending Other People's Money (OPM), we frequently give away our rights when we think they'll only impact Other People's Freedom (OPF).*

they hoped that reductions in liberty would only hurt "other" people. In the same way that government often gets away with spending on things that break natural laws because the citizens think it is spending Other People's Money (OPM), we frequently give away our rights when we think they'll only impact Other People's Freedom (OPF).

One of the most famous discussions about this law came from Christian pastor Martin Niemöller in his recollection of how Nazism spread in Germany and how few people did anything to stop its takeover of society. Pastor Niemöller is credited with saying:

First they came for the communists,
and I didn't speak out because I wasn't a communist.

Then they came for the socialists,
and I didn't speak out because I wasn't a socialist.

Then they came for the trade unionists,
and I didn't speak out because I wasn't a trade unionist.

Then they came for the Jews,
and I didn't speak out because I wasn't a Jew.

Then they came for me,
and there was no one left to speak for me.[2]

This is an excellent description of what happens when we ignorantly violate the law of liberty, allowing others to lose their rights while justifying that they probably deserved it and hoping it will never reach the point where it hurts us or those we love.

Note that Pastor Niemöller eventually became the leader of a group of clergymen opposed to Hitler and that he was arrested and held in Sachsenhausen and Dachau prison camps for the crime of not being "enthusiastic" about Nazism. Good for him! That's heroism. As Thoreau said, in a truly unjust society the only place for a really just man is in jail. Niemöller was later released by the Allies in 1945.

When a person loses freedom because he or she has caused harm to another person and arrest or imprisonment is needed to keep others safe or demand recompense for the harms to the victim, the loss of liberty is within the bounds of natural law. When a person is deprived of freedom for any other reason, it breaks natural law, and this hurts the entire society that allows such a violation of natural law.

Slavery is an obvious example. So is any kind of caste or class system where the laws and government treat a group of people differently because of their religion, race, gender, country of origin, beliefs, and so forth.

> *Those who truly understand freedom will stand up for the inalienable rights of all human beings from all walks of life.*

Those who truly understand freedom will stand up for the inalienable rights of all human beings from all walks of life because they realize that when others are free, their own freedom is safer, and when others lose their freedoms, their own freedom is always in jeopardy.

The Law of Maturity

A corollary of the law of freedom could be called the law of maturity, which teaches the levels of understanding freedom. The levels of maturity include (from worst to best):

Extreme Immaturity: The desire not to be free, to leave important decisions to others, and not have to live with the consequences of your choices and actions. The desire to have someone else take care of you.

High Immaturity: The desire to be free when it suits you but to leave many important decisions and the consequences of your actions to others; to get to do what you want but have someone else fix any problems that arise from your bad choices and actions.

Immaturity: The desire to be free and for others to be free, as long as the others are like you (same religion, race, gender, caste, nation, and so on) or are deemed to be "on your side" and the desire for those unlike you or not "on your side" to not have the same benefits "because they don't deserve them."

The desire to have the government treat you freely but treat "others" differently.

Low Maturity: The desire to be free and for all others to be free and to be forgiven when you are asked to account for your failures, while simultaneously wanting justice to be applied to others.

Moderate Maturity: The desire to be free in all situations, make your own decisions, and live with the consequences of your choices and actions and for others to do the same; to be free and accountable, and hope that others will do likewise.

High Maturity: The desire to be free and accountable and help all others enjoy the same; to take a stand and protect the inalienable rights and freedoms of all, including those who are different from you or are your enemies, even if this requires great personal sacrifices from you and those you love.

In historical times, most governments and nations have violated the law of liberty, which is a major reason that true freedom has been so rare in human experience. Governments and laws have withheld or taken away freedom from people based on their religion, beliefs, gender, race, ethnicity, nation of origin, disability, looks, words, ideas, friends, which books they had in their home, what religion they wanted to teach their children, and a number of other grounds that violated natural law.

Throughout history very few people have been willing to take an active stand for freedom when they were personally free but others were having their rights violated. This has occurred in too many ways and times to list, from the scared Christians who watched Jews slaughtered in Nazi Germany to the fearful Jews who watched Christians butchered in the Roman games, to otherwise good Americans who did nothing to stop the internment of patriotic Americans in the 1940s simply because they had Japanese ancestors or features.

Other examples include otherwise good Americans in the mid-nineteenth century who let women be raped, men be killed, and children be driven into the snow by American troops simply because of their Native American ethnicity or the otherwise good Americans who allowed slavery and later segregation to flourish in the American South based entirely on the color of people's skin.

Consequences of Breaking
the Law of Liberty

Human history is full of such violations of natural law, and in every case, the loss of freedom for the few has eventually decreased the level of freedom for all. When nations imprison their citizens because of their race, the same generation of officials always takes away the freedom of the majority in numerous ways. A government that allows slavery will always allow less freedom for the middle classes as well.

Find any government in history whose soldiers were allowed to rape and pillage with impunity, and you'll find a central government that was working behind the scenes to increase government power and reduce the freedoms of the people—rich, median, and poor alike. There are few, if any, exceptions to this principle in all of written history.

When a government is allowed to be unjust to one group, it establishes a precedent that all of us should carefully consider. Precedent is extremely powerful, either for good or bad. History has proven that even a good policy with a bad precedent will eventually lead to a bad policy.

For example, Caesar Augustus set a limit on taxes, but with this very action he created a precedent that the emperor had the power to establish tax levels. The Senate, which had the power to check this action, did nothing because the tax limit was low. But naturally, later emperors drastically raised taxes, and the Senate couldn't do anything because it had allowed the precedent of the emperor determining tax rates.

Similarly, in classical Greece, the Delian League allowed the great leader Aristides to single-handedly make numerous government decisions and set policies because they trusted him. He turned out to be worthy of the trust, and the people flourished. A few years later he retired, and his replacements for many years afterward abused the power of the office. The policy of allowing Aristides to make choices turned out well as long as he was in office, but the precedent of giving one man so much power inevitably backfired. This is one of the examples George Washington looked to when he refused to be king.

Any government that allows a loss of freedom for some is also planning or implementing additional ways to expand its power over other groups of people (or soon will).

No matter how much a nation may think that it is okay to withhold freedom from any group of people (except in the case of crime), the precedent of doing so limits the freedom of everyone. The law of liberty is real. Any government that allows a loss of freedom for some is also planning or implementing additional ways to expand its power over other groups of people (or soon will).

Consequences Today

In our day, this should give pause to any caring and wise citizen. A nation that allows the termination of unborn babies and withholds the freedom of opportunity from immigrants (not for defense, but on the basis of "keeping others out of our country") is, according to the law of liberty, violating natural law in other ways.

This may be occurring in secret labs, with the training of troops to go door to door and subdue a populace in its own nation, or in various other plans hatched behind closed doors, but the law of liberty guarantees that something like these things is happening. For example, it is natural that a nation that interned its patriotic citizens of Japanese descent was simultaneously establishing the biggest complex of secret government operations in all of history. Indeed, many of the same national leaders were in charge of both.

In fact, to know what level of secrecy is currently being applied by a modern government, those who understand the law of freedom only need to look at how much that government stands for the freedom of all versus withholding freedom from some groups—whatever the reasons.

Liberty and Justice Come from Indivisible Freedom

Freedom is indivisible in the long term, and only societies that are consistently spreading freedom to more people are trustworthy behind the scenes. Even more importantly, the attitude of the people is a clear indicator of the future of freedom. A nation of people that wants to withhold the opportunities of freedom from any group(s)—including immigrants—is likely to elect officials who will perpetuate governments based on secrecy and power rather than transparency and honest freedom for all.

The law of liberty is a wake-up call to all modern nations. When any group is being treated with suspicion by government or allowed to have fewer freedoms than the majority, the government is not to be fully trusted, and all the people's freedoms are in jeopardy.

If this uncomfortable reality hits too close to home in your nation, you know that the law of liberty is probably being violated. The most effective and immediate solution is to look around, find a group that is being denied its rights and opportunities, and help take a stand for freedom—even if you aren't part of this group. When freedom is unjustly lost for some, it is lost for all of us. Any injustice reduces our liberty.

CHAPTER 11

THE LAW OF ECONOMY

ALL POWERS DELEGATED TO GOVERNMENT MUST BE ENTRUSTED
TO THE LOWEST LEVEL OF GOVERNMENT THAT CAN EFFECTIVELY
ACCOMPLISH THE DESIRED GOAL; NATIONS THAT ADHERE TO THIS
PRINCIPLE ARE CONSISTENTLY STRONG, VIGOROUS, AND VIBRANT.

J ames Madison said that if men were angels, manmade government would be unnecessary.[1] Likewise, if God ran our governments, centralization of all powers would be fine. As an omni-
scient, omnipotent, benevolent, and perfectly just being, He would
ensure that everything was governed flawlessly. But since men and
women run our government institutions, we should be careful to give
them only the powers they truly need and should have—and then to
closely watch them lest they abuse their powers.

As Madison put it, "In framing
a government which is to be
administered by men over men,
the great difficulty lies in this: you
must first enable the government to
control the governed; and in the next
place oblige it to control itself."[2] The larger the government, the more
difficult this is.

> *Bigger governments
> always take away more
> freedom than they did
> when they were smaller.*

Bigger governments always take away more freedom than they
did when they were smaller. As institutions get bigger and bigger,
they become more complex. When government gets larger, it becomes

more difficult to keep it checked within the bounds of its constitution. If it becomes extremely large, the level of government abuse, spending, and overreach is the greatest of all historical threats to the freedom of the people.

Such overgrown governments have arisen a number of times in history, and as we mentioned earlier, it is the nature of government to expand its control as widely as possible. Thomas Jefferson warned of this very concern when he said, "The way to have good and safe government is not to trust it all to one, but to divide it among the many, distributing to every one exactly the functions he is competent to [perform best]."[3] Note that he was speaking here of different levels of government. In the very next sentence, he continued:

> Let the national government be entrusted with the defense of the nation, and its foreign and federal relations; the State governments with the civil rights, law, police, and administration of what concerns the state generally; the counties with the local concerns of the counties, and the ward [township] direct the interests within itself.
>
> It is by dividing and subdividing these republics, from the great national one down through all its subordinations, until it ends in the administration of every man's [home and business] by himself; by placing under every one his own eye may superintend, that all will be done for the best.
>
> What has destroyed liberty and the rights of man in every government which has ever existed under the sun? The generalizing and concentrating all cares and powers into one body, no matter whether of the autocrats of Russia or France, or of the aristocrats of a Venetian state.[4]

Why Governments Decline

James Madison taught the same principle in *Federalist* 45, and it was discussed at length in the founding era. Note that Jefferson said very clearly that this centralizing of power into big government has been the thing that "destroyed liberty and the rights of man in every government which has ever existed." No exceptions.

Some people have argued that by centralizing most of the power in one big government—at the national or even global level—we can create a government that is extremely efficient and more effective than others. But all human experience has shown the opposite. Bigger governments have always taken away more freedom from the people than those that are, in Jefferson's words, "divided and subdivided."

> *The very definition of freedom is having the liberty to do the things you want and choose within the realm of your areas of stewardship.*

The very definition of freedom is having the liberty to do the things you want and choose within the realm of your areas of stewardship. When a national or global government begins meddling with how people do business and run their homes, freedom quickly declines. Also, when a national (or global) government overreaches, the natural result is that state, provincial, county, and local governments tend to do the same.

The key, as Jefferson and Madison outlined, is for each level of government, starting with individuals, to do what they can do best at the lowest level. So families should govern their own homes, and communities should govern everything that can be effectively handled at the local level.

If there is something that affects several communities, a larger city might be called upon to oversee it, and a county may be asked to govern something that touches a number of cities. Following this same pattern, the state or province should have only the power to do things that require a consistent policy for multiple counties.

The Role of Federal Governments

The result of this approach is that the only things for national governments to do are (1) protect from foreign attacks, (2) negotiate trade on behalf of all the states and provinces together, (3) help decide disputes between states or provinces, and (4) ensure that lower governments are protecting the inalienable rights of all citizens regardless of religion, race, gender, ethnicity, disability, or any other consideration. Everything else can be more effectively, wisely, and economically handled at lower levels.

If modern nations were to apply this one logical and obvious principle, most of the problems caused by governments around the world would disappear. And freedom, free enterprise, opportunity for all, and widespread prosperity would become the norm.

As historian John Fiske wrote in 1916:

> If the day should ever arrive (which God forbid!) when the people of different parts of our country shall allow their local affairs to be administered by prefects sent from Washington, and when the self-government of the states shall have been so far lost as those of the departments of France, or even so closely limited as that of the counties of England—on that day the political career of the American people will have been robbed of its most interesting and valuable features, and the usefulness of this nation will be lamentably impaired.[5]

Today, the government in Washington is much more controlling of states and counties than the governments of 1916 France and England mentioned by Fiske were. Moreover, the scope of things that Washington regulates is constantly increasing. At the same time, many modern nations including France, England, Canada, Germany, and others are following this same pattern.

The Proper Place for Power

Natural law is clear. Government should only govern what the people need it to govern, at the lowest level that it can do so effectively. This principle is simple and economical: Keep the power at the lowest effective level. Any delegation of power to a level of government above what is needed is wasteful, and it always leads to loss of freedoms.

The closer the power of government is to the people it is supposed to serve, the more likely it is that it will not overstep its bounds, and the easier it is for the people to put an abusive government or official back in line.

The strength of central government is more resources against external threats, which is why national governments are best for defense.

The strength of local governance is higher levels of internal peace and prosperity. This is why the American founding fathers set up a mixed government, with national defense run from the federal government and the rest controlled more locally. Every move away from this focus has decreased the freedom of the people.

> *The strength of local governance is higher levels of internal peace and prosperity.*

Another strength of keeping powers at the lowest possible level is that governments make better decisions when the stakeholders (the people government serves) are more closely involved in the decision making as well as daily implementation. The further the officials are from those they serve, the less likely they are to efficiently and effectively make excellent governing choices.

This principle is neither complex nor difficult to apply. Yet it is widely ignored for two main reasons. First, the aristocratic, elitist, and authoritarian elements in society would lose most of their power under such a system, so they invest large amounts of money and influence to push for the centralization of power into bigger and bigger governments. As government size increases, those who can significantly influence the government become wealthier and more powerful—which will eventually lead to rule by a global elite unless current trends change.

Second, when ordinary people see themselves as too busy to get involved in daily governance, they simply let their freedoms be taken away. This usually happens slowly, so the people don't notice. In times of crisis, it happens more quickly. Note that most people don't mean to lose freedom, but they don't focus significant time or energy on keeping it.

Natural law requires those who most benefit from freedom, the citizenry, to stand up for it—or lose it. Most elites aren't very concerned about protecting freedom for the masses because the super-rich tend to have a lot of freedom in all societies, even when the large majority of people lose their liberties. If the people don't work hard specifically to keep their freedom, they lose it. This has become a law of history, and it is a huge reality in the world today.

CHAPTER 12

THE LAW OF PROGRESS

THE ACTUAL LEVEL OF FREEDOM AND PROSPERITY IN ANY SOCIETY
IS DIRECTLY EQUIVALENT TO THE LEVEL OF FREE ENTERPRISE.

I t is the nature of human beings to progress. When they achieve any goal, they almost immediately start planning toward the next one. Put simply, people want to succeed. They don't all agree on what success is, or which areas of success are most important, but nearly everyone wants some kind of success. Most people also want progress—where there is increased opportunity for everyone.

Throughout history, nearly all success and progress have come from enterprise, which consists of taking action toward goals. Unfortunately, humankind has always found that there are various barriers to the things they want to accomplish. Some of the barriers are natural and come from the physical world we live in. Others are manmade, meaning that other people make certain goals more difficult to attain.

Some barriers to success are internal and must be overcome by the individual facing his or her inner challenges. All of these barriers are part of life, and success and progress usually come only after struggling against such roadblocks and finding ways past, around, over, under, or through them.

Sadly, governments sometimes create the worst barriers of all. When this occurs, the government shuts down success and progress, or at the very least, it makes these things much more difficult. This is particularly bad because the purpose of government, the very reason it was established in the first place, is to remove two of the biggest barriers in life—plunder from domestic and international attacks.

Sometimes government becomes a bigger barrier than the things it was created to protect against. In such cases, as James Madison put it in *Federalist* 10, the remedy (government) is worse than the disease (attacks on inalienable rights). When the government becomes a hindrance to enterprise, it is the enemy of both success and progress.

Enterprise Is Better

Under free enterprise, societies make better decisions. This occurs simply because individuals tend to choose better for themselves than government officials. While of course some individuals do make bad decisions, the truth remains that in most cases, a person is more qualified than a government to choose for his or her needs.

Orrin Woodward shared the following example: If a family selects a cable TV company or online provider, they can easily change it next month if it is lacking in service, quality, or other important factors. They naturally adjust and fix it immediately and effectively—or they keep adjusting until they get what serves them best. In contrast, once a government selects a cable company for a person or town, it takes a great deal of effort, cost, and usually conflict to change companies. And it nearly always takes a long time.

Woodward further shared the example of a man who has one hand in a fire and the other in a bucket of ice. Free enterprise allows the man to immediately adjust, pull his hands out of harm, and use the warmth of one to heat the other and the icy hand to cool his burns. In contrast, if a government official or czar is in charge, the individual has to lobby, convince, campaign, and argue to get his hands moved.

Moreover, the government tends to deal with such situations by using statistics, which will show that while one hand is hot, the other is cold, and the average is basically a balance. "The state of the union in this matter is good," the bureaucratic view will determine from the statistics. "Very balanced. Change nothing."

Yet the man ends up with both burns and frostbite. When the government applies the law of averages and proclaims that everyone is well, it hurts freedom and progress. The businessman with his hands in fire and ice is left to either burn and freeze or to do what makes business sense and risk breaking the law.

In short, free enterprise decentralizes the decision making to the lowest possible level, so better decisions are more frequent. As a result, society experiences increased progress.

> *In short, free enterprise decentralizes the decision making to the lowest possible level, so better decisions are more frequent. As a result, society experiences increased progress.*

How Governments Break the Law of Progress

Again, the biggest roadblock to individual success and societal progress occurs when government impedes enterprise. There are several specific ways in which the government does this. Note that all of these occur when government attempts to do more than protect its citizens' inalienable rights, trying to do things no citizen could legitimately or morally do alone under natural law. Such government actions include:

- Doing anything not allowed by natural law

- Operating under a constitution not agreed upon by the people

- Doing anything not allowed by the nation's constitution

- Fixing prices for any reason other than an act of war

- Fixing wages for any reason other than an act of war

- Controlling production or businesses for any reason other than an act of war or to prevent attacks on the inalienable rights of citizens

- Granting monopolies

- Requiring licenses or special permits for any reason other than an act of war or to prevent attacks on inalienable rights of the citizens

- Subsidizing certain products or businesses

- Giving money or a special benefit to some people while withholding it from others

- Spending more than it has

- Borrowing money for any reason beyond national security

- Printing inflationary money, which hurts the lower and middle classes because their spending power decreases

Note that all of these things drastically impact the economy and have a negative effect on enterprise. Specifically, when a government engages in any of these behaviors, it increases the roadblocks to enterprise and decreases the amount of success and progress.

"Free" Enterprise

When the government does none these things, or anything else beyond its role of protecting the inalienable rights of the people, enterprise is free to do what it chooses. As long as individuals and businesses don't violate the inalienable rights of others, they can use this freedom to pursue happiness and achieve their goals.

This system, known as "free enterprise," offers the most opportunity for the most people and results in the highest levels of economic opportunity, widespread prosperity, and freedom for all. The two fundamental principles of free enterprise are that the government must (1) protect the inalienable rights of everyone and (2) treat everyone the same before the law.

In such a system, people are free to seek and achieve whatever success they desire (again, as long as it doesn't violate the inalienable rights of others). When all people have such incentives, the whole society experiences great levels of progress.

When free enterprise is allowed to exist, the people flourish economically, and freedom spreads to more people. The power of any nation using free enterprise greatly increases. In contrast, when free enterprise is weakened by the government, for any reason, freedom declines. So do economic success and progress for the majority of people.

> *In such a system, people are free to seek and achieve whatever success they desire (again, as long as it doesn't violate the inalienable rights of others). When all people have such incentives, the whole society experiences great levels of progress.*

A lot more has been said about the principle of free enterprise, but too often the commentaries obscure the simple reality that freedom requires free enterprise. Free enterprise occurs when the government protects inalienable rights, treating everyone equally, and does nothing else.

Test Your Government

Try a simple test to determine how much freedom (and free enterprise) your nation currently has. Mark each of the following that your government does:

____ Does your government do anything not allowed by natural law (such as take money from some and give it to others for nonmilitary purposes, treat those belonging to any race or religion differently than those of any other, or regulate individuals or businesses in ways that have nothing to do with national security or protecting the inalienable rights of others, etc.)?

____ Does your government do anything not allowed by the nation's constitution (such as send troops to war without an official declaration of war) or do things at the national level that the constitution says should be done at a lower level?

____ Does your government fix prices for any reason other than an act of war?

____ Does your government fix wages for any reason other than an act of war?

____ Does your government control production or businesses for any reason other than an act of war or to prevent attacks on the inalienable rights of citizens?

____ Does your government grant or support monopolies?

____ Does your government ever require licenses or special permits for any reason other than an act of war or to prevent attacks on the inalienable rights of citizens?

____ Does your government ever subsidize certain products or businesses?

____ Does your government ever give money or a special benefit to some people while withholding it from others?

____ Does your government ever spend more than it has?

____ Does your government ever borrow money for any reason beyond national security?

____ Does your government ever print inflationary money?

Count up how many items you marked, and see where your nation is in the process of losing freedom.

Stage 1: If your government does one or two of these, you should be concerned that it is headed in the direction of less freedom. Of course, if it used to do more of these in the recent past and now is doing fewer of them, it is at least going in the right direction.

Stage 2: If your government does three to six of these, you are definitely living in a time of decreasing freedom. Even if your nation used to do more of these in the past and is now heading in the right direction, it is still essential to keep a close eye on things.

Stage 3: If your government does seven to nine of these things, the inertia away from freedom is very strong, and only major times of crisis will bring opportunities to turn things around.

Stage 4: If your government does ten to twelve of these, it is time for all members of your nation to get deeply serious about learning the principles of natural law and get involved in applying them. This will take significant effort from you and many others, and it is essential to get started immediately. Times of crisis will come soon (because this decrease of freedom always causes major problems), and you need to be prepared to help turn things in the right direction at a time when more people are looking for answers.

Note that the United States, which has long stood as a symbol of freedom in the world, is firmly in Stage 4. While this is cause for serious concern to American citizens, they should also be enthusiastic that times of great change are just ahead. They should do their best to prepare to help society turn in the right direction soon. In the meantime, nothing is more important than teaching people the principles of natural law and using what free enterprise still exists to engage in entrepreneurial projects.

To be even more specific, two things will turn a nation around:

1. More people who understand and apply natural law and who read the great books and ideas and every important book they can get their hands on

2. More entrepreneurs who gain leadership and resources and build teams of committed people who want to improve themselves and the world

Two Enterprises

We can call these the "reading enterprise" and the "business enterprise." When you do both of these, you become a leader for freedom.

Leaders are readers, and freedom requires entrepreneurial thinking, creativity, innovation, initiative, tenacity, and ingenuity. The law of progress says that all success and progress come from enterprise, and when enterprise is free, more people have increased opportunity, prosperity, and liberty.

The ordinary people of our nation, and of all nations, are capable of amazing things. Most of them work hard, love their families, love God, and care about the future of freedom, morality, and opportunity. But more is needed. Free people must work to keep their freedoms, to make sure that their enterprises (at home and in the workplace) remain free.

If governments continue to intervene in our homes, jobs, and the economy, freedom and opportunities to pursue happiness will keep decreasing.

Almost everyone wants our children and grandchildren to live in a world where their freedom and standard of living are even better than ours, but if we continue on the current path, the opposite will be true. Today, most Americans believe their children will have a worse lifestyle than they do. The solution to this challenge is free enterprise, the backbone of success and progress.

> *Free people must work to keep their freedoms, to make sure that their enterprises (at home and in the workplace) remain free.*

Real Solutions

Fortunately, each of us has real power to increase free enterprise. The natural laws covered in this book are real, and they work. To the extent that we apply them, we will succeed. To the extent that we don't, we will decline.

You can apply these twelve natural laws, and by doing so, you will set an example for others. You can help other people learn about them, until every person in your nation has heard of these laws and had the chance to apply them.

The future of freedom and prosperity for your children and grandchildren literally depends on how well you and all of us in this generation understand and apply these natural laws.

KNOWLEDGE IS POWER

"How's the weather there?" I asked as soon as he answered the phone.

"Sunny and a balmy seventy-nine degrees," he responded cheerfully. "I'm in my office at the computer, and I can see the bay through my window. There's a light breeze, and the waves are lapping against the dock. Why do you ask?"

> *If we can just adopt a few of these in our nation, it will improve everything. These are the problems we're facing today, and applying these twelve laws is* exactly *what is needed to fix the nation.*

"You're killing me, man," I said with feeling. "There's two feet of snow outside, and we can't get our cars up the steep driveway. The older kids have been shoveling snow for hours."

He chuckled and then said, "That's why we love Florida! You should come visit."

"Today or tomorrow?" I asked.

After we both stopped laughing, I said, "The ski slopes are full, though!"

"I'm glad you called," he said, getting down to business. "I just finished reading through your last chapter, and I have a few ideas."

"Great." I opened my notebook to a blank page. "That's why I called."

"Well, first let me say I am glad you wrote this book. It is vital information for citizens and leaders. Our society desperately needs this right now."

"But have we effectively communicated just how important natural law is?" I asked.

"I hope so. I'm sure of one thing: These twelve are the perfect natural laws to begin with. If we can just adopt a few of these in our nation, it will improve everything. These are the problems we're facing today, and applying these twelve laws is *exactly* what is needed to fix the nation."

"I keep worrying that the chapters are too short," I said. "What do you think?" I could tell he must have gone outside because I could now hear the waves hitting the dock on the other end of the line.

"Not at all. You're not writing to some ivory-tower scholar or to a politician who likes long, complex documents. You're writing to the regular people in America and around the world who care about freedom and want to know what will actually fix their national problems.

"This is perfect for that. It's short, hard-hitting, and to the point. It doesn't pull punches, and it focuses on the most relevant natural laws for our time. Don't ruin it by making it longer."

"That makes sense." I turned the space heater up a notch to take the chill out of the room. "There's just so much more we could say about each of these twelve natural laws, and we could add in another twenty or more to make it more thorough. But you're right; it's about really getting the message to the people."

"Exactly. We want everyone to read it—as many people as possible. And then we want them to do something about it, to take action. If it is any bigger, it will be like countless books that people start reading, put on a shelf, and never apply to real life.

"Your focus shouldn't be on outlining every natural law that is important to government but rather the few, key natural laws that are needed right now to fix our specific national problems. These twelve do that!"

"Okay, so what are your concerns with the book?"

"I'll email you the small editing suggestions," he replied, "but here's my big question. How are you going to conclude this book?"

"Well, I can't just tell them to go out and influence elections," I said. "People who care about freedom have been doing that for decades, and it's not working."

"And it won't," he said firmly. "You and I both know that the forces of decline are too strong right now. The law of inertia has created too much momentum, so the normal options like elections aren't going to fix our problems. They're still important, but not nearly as important right now as these twelve laws."

"Agreed. But unless we can get ordinary people involved, nothing is going to change. We need the citizens to stand up and lead, or we can all kiss the American Dream good-bye."

"I wouldn't say it exactly that way because I don't think *all* the people are going to suddenly awaken and magically begin to lead. I do believe we need a lot more people to stand up and get much more involved in influencing our nation—*a lot more.* And if it doesn't happen soon, it will be too late, like you said. But we only need a few, the 5 percent rather than the 95 percent."

> *Unless we can get ordinary people involved, nothing is going to change. We need the citizens to stand up and lead, or we can all kiss the American Dream good-bye.*

"Good point. It will only take some of the people to really turn things in the right direction. Not *every* citizen, or even a majority, but just a number who are truly committed. I mean, a lot really care about freedom already, but we need a lot more who understand these natural laws to help spread them far and wide."

I switched my phone to the other ear. "These twelve laws are powerful. If more people knew them—a *lot* more, millions of people— things would drastically improve."

"That's true," he affirmed. "If millions knew these twelve simple natural laws, it would have a huge impact on freedom."

"So is this a book millions will want to read?"

"If they hear about it, yes. It's exactly the fix we've all been waiting for—and I mean the whole nation. These twelve natural laws are that powerful. They are. We just need to get them out there," he said.

"And tell everyone who reads this to make sure they get a copy into the hands of everyone who cares about the future," I added. "Freedom *matters,* and these twelve laws *matter.*" I paused. "It feels strange to have the answers to fixing the nation's problems in our hands and just pray and hope that enough people will read this. If they do, it will have a powerful chance to fix things."

He said firmly, "Knowledge is power. Let's get this knowledge out to everyone we can reach."

After a short silence, I began laughing.

"What's funny?" he asked.

"I was just thinking that we've got the conclusion," I replied.

"We do? What do you mean?"

"We need the readers to provide the conclusion for the book, not me. I mean, the only real conclusion to a book on these twelve incredibly powerful natural laws is for the people to pass this book on—far and wide.

"Okay, maybe this is a little out there. But what if I just told the readers about this? What if I just told them that the only way to finish this book is to get this message out, to help other people realize that these twelve natural laws are the solution to our problems?"

"We could just ask them to help," he said.

"I agree. And how many do you think will follow through and do something to help?" I asked.

He pondered. "I think it depends on how specific you are. What exactly do you want them to do?"

I responded immediately: "To give this book to at least two other people and tell them it is the solution to America's problems, and they really need to read it."

He agreed, "After all, we have the problems we do in our nation precisely because most of the people don't know these laws. They really don't. And until they do, nothing is going to change."

I continued the thread. "It's true. Everything in our society is a result of the principles that determine our outcomes. And having a shared vision of the principles of freedom will determine the type of society we create. As long as we continue to ignore these higher laws, we're going to just keep experiencing one crisis and setback after another. But if the knowledge of these twelve natural laws gets to enough people, we'll fix our political problems."

"Yes," he said. "And the sooner the better. Until a lot more people understand these twelve . . . well, you already said it."

After a brief silence, I said, "This will work."

"Yes, it will. Many people want to fix things, and it will work in two ways.

"First, if this is how the book ends, people will get two or more copies and give them to other people who care about freedom. And second, if enough people learn these twelve natural laws, they will change the future."

Thinking again about the warm breeze and Florida sunshine he was enjoying, I shouldered my coat and went to check on the progress of the snow removal.

Far to the north, from Philadelphia to New York to Ottawa, the day was clear and cold, causing people to hurry from taxis into tall buildings. The snowstorm that had left fresh powder in the towns and slopes of the Rockies made its way across the plains and into the Midwest.

Men removed their coats in the heat of wedding parties in Dallas and Charleston. Rain fell from Portland to Vancouver and all the way up to Anchorage, while surfers in wetsuits enjoyed larger-than-seasonal swells on California beaches.

If enough people learn these twelve natural laws, they will change the future.

Their compatriots on Ka'anapali Beach in Maui also noted that the waves were pretty big today. All over the continent, people enjoyed their freedom and the lives it afforded them.

A few of them, at that very moment, were thinking about freedom. Some were reading; others were engaged in raising their families or building their businesses. Most didn't realize that the future hangs on twelve natural laws.

But it does.

OUR INVITATION TO YOU

Please share this book and spread these twelve natural laws far and wide. Knowledge is power, and these twelve natural laws are the fix to our national problems.

Government isn't likely to fix things, nor will we likely see much real change from politicians or big institutions.

If things are going to be fixed, it is up to ordinary people. The people need to know these twelve natural laws.

Please give a copy of this book to at least two other people.

Please go online, tell at least twenty people about this book, and encourage them to read it.

Will you help us?

A Brief History of Natural Law

ALL LEGISLATION IS BASED ON NATURAL LAW, AND IF IT CONTRADICTS
NATURAL LAW, THAT LEGISLATION CANNOT BE VALID.
—NICHOLAS OF CUSA, A.D. 1401–1464

BEFORE FRANKLIN ROOSEVELT, WE HAD THE REPUBLIC (CHECKS AND
BALANCES, LIMITED GOVERNMENT, INALIENABLE RIGHTS TO LIBERTY
AND PROPERTY, AND ALL THAT). AFTER 1933 WE BEGAN TO GET THE
CENTRALIZED STATE AND INTERVENTIONIST CONTROLS OF INDUSTRY.
ACTUALLY, HOWEVER, THE INNER SPIRIT OF THE OLD AMERICA HAD BEEN
HOLLOWED OUT IN THE TWENTIES. THE COLLEGES HAD CEASED TO TEACH
ANYTHING IMPORTANT ABOUT OUR HERITAGE. YOU HAD TO BE A GRADUATE
STUDENT TO CATCH UP WITH THE *FEDERALIST* PAPERS . . . OR WITH *THE
WEALTH OF NATIONS*. WE WERE THE IGNORANT GENERATION.
—JOHN CHAMBERLAIN

In historical times, an epic debate raged about which kind of law was supreme—scientific versus revealed laws. But both revealed and scientific laws are part of natural law, and both are above manmade laws.

In the modern world, all natural laws (scientific, revealed, moral, political, etc.) are often seen as less important than manmade laws. Governments are considered supreme by many people, and this is both a misunderstanding of natural law and an excuse to ignore the natural laws that govern the universe and politics.

All this has led to a loss of freedom and a decline of nations in the free world. It has also caused deep and frequently painful divisions in our societies, because those who believe in a higher law and those who believe in the supremacy of manmade laws and governments have stopped speaking to each other in the shared and civil language of natural law.

Blue versus red states, doves versus hawks, interventionists versus isolationists, statists versus free enterprisers, liberals versus conservatives, party versus party, various religions versus each other, skeptics versus believers, atheists versus Christians—the discontent and even hatred that people in these groups often show toward each other are symptomatic of this loss of a common language.

When a large portion of our society believes in higher laws, while another large group believes in the supremacy of manmade laws, there is little shared vision, and the dialogue grows increasingly strident and angry. This division has reached the point where the sides seldom listen to each other; instead, each bands together in like-minded cliques to denigrate the other. If this trend continues, widespread ideologically-based violence will likely result, and decline is certain.

The Power of a Common Language

Natural law is a solution. Both sides, all sides, of the Great Conversation over time are rooted in the traditions of natural law. It is time to recover this tradition, to bring it into the national conversation about political ideas, and to use it to civilize the debates and passions that divide us.

Jefferson was doing exactly this when he appealed to both sides of the debate with the phrase "nature and nature's God" at the beginning of the Declaration of Independence.

Our generation needs a similar return to wisdom.

Ideals and Fairness

Plato taught that there is a perfect Ideal of justice and fairness, and that it is above humankind. Humans and manmade institutions attempt, hopefully, to achieve this ideal, and it is the same ideal for all human societies at all times in history.

C. S. Lewis wrote about the moral laws that govern the universe and all people in it: "Wherever you find a man who says he does not believe in a real Right and Wrong, you will find the same man going back on this a moment later. He may break his promise to you, but if you try breaking one to him, he will be complaining 'It's not fair' before you can say 'Jack Robinson.'"

Lewis continued. "If no set of moral ideas were truer or better than any other, there would be no sense in preferring . . . Christian morality to Nazi morality. . . . If your moral ideas can be truer, and those of the Nazis less true, there must be something—some real morality—for them to be true about."

The fact that we can compare different morals and laws means that there is something to compare them to, some higher standard against which all systems of human law can be measured.

This supreme law is what Plato called the Universal Ideal, the yardstick against which all laws, governments, and cultural traditions are evaluated. And people do it naturally, without even meaning to, especially as they talk about what is fair or unfair. Indeed, when our mothers admonished us that "life isn't fair," they were actually saying that the people we deal with in life don't always follow natural law— even though they should.

Every society must be governed by truths that nearly everyone in the society agrees upon. Historically these truths surrounded the local deities and faith of the people. Hellenic Greece and imperial Rome were confronted with the same situation facing North America and Europe today: How do people of a multitude of faiths and systems of belief operate within the same system? Since the individual faiths and viewpoints see the world differently, how do we find "common ground" in order to live in a just and free society?

The answer from Aristotle onward, including the Stoics, was that civilizations could have a multitude of faiths and belief systems but find common ground within natural laws. These laws are built within the structure of human beings and are conspicuous in every historical society. In fact, even when these laws were violated, the people knew they were being violated. This has often been referred to as "common sense."

Rules of the Road

When society identifies the common ground of natural law, liberty is increased as all parties buy into the rules of law. For instance, Orrin Woodward said:

> Imagine if a society rejected the "rules of the road." You may want to drive on the right side, but another driver wants to drive on the left side. Others alternate which side they drive on based upon the direction they are driving or a flip of the coin— or just their mood today, and their different mood tomorrow.
>
> "Madness," you say? "Chaos"? In the same way, if there is not a set of common laws or rules that everyone buys into, freedom is lost by all. Without such rules, chaos ensues and no one dares drive on the road unless they have a big enough vehicle to run over everyone else. For example, would you send your teenage daughter to the store on an errand if other drivers just drove as they want without rules?
>
> Rules of the road actually create liberty—instead of hinder it—when everyone buys into a few basic guidelines.

In the same way, when everyone in society buys into a few easily understood and inherent guidelines of humanity that have been written into our DNA as natural law, then life becomes simpler, and liberty is possible.

And as the agreed-upon rules more closely conform to natural law, life and liberty improve, and the pursuit of happiness becomes easier.

Consequently, rule of natural law is essential for society to have ordered liberty, and without it, society will sway to the extreme left (license) or to the extreme right (forcing people to obey what they don't believe). The right shift can be any form of totalitarianism where people are told what to believe and how to act with the threat of consequences for noncompliance, and the left shift becomes so libertine that eventually there are no laws except that the strong rule over the weak.

In other words, the extremes of both left and right eventually bring the same negative results. Only rule of natural law flows with human nature without violating biblical and other moral principles, and natural law is the basis of the best teachings of all religions, philosophies, and systems of belief. In fact, the best ideas are good precisely because they are built on natural law.

Natural versus Positive Law

There are two major traditions of law in human history: natural law and positive law. As we've already discussed, natural law is made up of all laws that are above humankind and that humanity cannot control or change. Positive law, in contrast, consists of all manmade laws, including decrees by kings and presidents, statutes voted into law by congresses and parliaments, and treaties entered into between nations.

Another form of positive law is the creation of constitutions, which consist of guidelines and laws that govern the actions of governments.

The term *positive* means law that is posited, or made, by humans, as compared to natural law, which has always existed.[1] In other words, people posit or create positive law, but we can only *discover* natural law.

Note that there are really two types of positive law. The first, the pure positive law view, is based on the idea that manmade law is truly supreme. From this perspective, force is the most powerful thing in the world, and governments through history have been able to project more force than anything else, so manmade government is the supreme power in the world. It follows that if government is the supreme entity, it must fix every problem and right every wrong. There is nothing such a government shouldn't attempt to do for good according to this view, so there are no limits on the role of government.

When the idea of natural law comes up, pure positivists respond that there is no absolute proof that any natural law exists or that anything besides force really has power in the world. In this view, money has value in that it increases power, but power is the ultimate goal.

The second kind of positive law, what the great natural law scholar Heinrich Rommen referred to as *methodological* positivism, accepts that natural law is real and that all manmade laws must conform to and support natural law. Only manmade governments and laws that are in concert with natural law are truly positive in this view, and the only way to have progress in a society is for all manmade laws to follow the higher laws.

Clearly, these two branches of positivism are opposites. In fact, when we refer to those who support natural law, we include the methodological positivists in this group. They believe that we should combine natural law with the best lessons of history and continually attempt to improve our laws and governments. This second kind of positivism is really just another way of describing the natural law worldview.[2]

The Oxford and University of Turin scholar A. P. d'Entrèves gave a series of lectures on natural law at the University of Chicago in 1948, and his work was later collected in a book entitled simply *Natural Law*. In the Hutchinson University Library edition of this book, he outlined three types of positive law that differ from Rommen's two types.

The three types include imperativism, which is manmade law that people must follow, such as decrees by a king. A second type, realism, occurs where those writing the law try to carefully construct the law in such a way that it will be upheld by the courts. The third kind of positive law, according to d'Entrèves, is normativism, where the focus is creating a body of interconnected laws that together serve to push society in the direction it should go.[3]

Different writers and thinkers through history have used various terms for the opposite of natural law, including the following: positive law, civil law, municipal law, written law, manmade law, man's law, or human law.[4] These all refer to manmade laws, and all are bound by natural law. Of course, the true opposite of natural law is anything that contradicts or breaks it.[5]

Montesquieu—the writer most quoted by the American framers during the Constitutional Convention of 1789—wrote, "Before laws were made, there were relations of possible justice. To say that there is nothing just or unjust but what is commanded or forbidden by positive laws, is the same as saying that before the describing of a circle all radii were not equal."

John Locke agreed and wrote, "The law of nature stands as an eternal rule to all men, legislators as well as others." And man's laws "are only so far right as they are founded on the law of nature, by which they are to be regulated and interpreted."[6]

Natural Law in Scripture and Literature

Still, despite such clear reasoning on the existence of natural law, throughout history, there has been an ongoing battle about which is supreme—natural law or manmade laws. The battle between Pharaoh and Moses in the Bible is one of the earliest portrayals of this conflict. Pharaoh, convinced that a monarch's laws are supreme, faced major tragedy as he unsuccessfully attempted to circumvent higher laws.

Even those who don't believe in deity can see how the biblical writers attempted to teach this lesson, not just in the case of Pharaoh but repeatedly in the stories of Adam and Eve, the people in Noah's time, Abraham and his posterity, King David, and so on. Kings and leaders in the Bible faced the recurring theme of pitting human strength against higher laws—and losing.

Other classics of human civilization taught the same lesson, from the stories of Homer and mythology to the failed attempt of Socrates to convince the Athenians to put natural law above human governments. The poet Sophocles pitted kingly power against natural law in the Oedipus trilogy and showed that, without question, there are higher natural laws that govern all humanity and manmade institutions. Sophocles actually used the phrase "the eternal and unwritten law."[7]

The early Greek thinkers sought for the supreme law of the universe. Thales thought the scientific laws of water held the answers to all things,[8] and Pythagoras taught that mathematical laws held the keys to understanding all natural laws.[9] Heraclitus proposed that never-ending change was the ultimate law, and "Parmenides declared that being, rather than becoming, was the basic principle."[10]

But as scientists and philosophers learned more, they put aside older views and began to explore the relationship between the laws of nature and the moral/political idea of justice.[11]

Plato's dialogues outline many of these Greek debates about natural law. For example, Socrates and Protagoras argued about whether humans learn natural law from their inherent reason or just by what they are taught by society.[12] Socrates argued strongly that natural law is inherent in people and not merely a reflection of whatever any given society decides to teach its youth.

In two other dialogues, Socrates argued against those who believe that the strong should rule over the weak and that the supreme law is determined by those with the most power.[13] This same view was rekindled in modern times by Friedrich Nietzsche, who suggested that a morality based on right and wrong is weak and should be replaced by a morality of the strong over the weak.

The natural law viewpoint, with Socrates, holds that there are laws above humankind that are binding upon the weak and the strong, as well as on both good people and bad. Socrates taught, at least according to Plato's account, that higher ideals of goodness and truth are the measure of all things done by humanity. People achieve happiness and virtue only by conforming to the natural laws.

The writer Virgil tried to warn Rome of its impending decline and suggested the vital need to return to compliance with natural law. These early great classics—the Bible, *Iliad*, *Odyssey*, *Aeneid*, and so forth—emphasize the thesis of natural law as supreme. And Thomas More's famous face-off against King Henry VIII teaches the same story: human law versus natural law and the ultimate supremacy of the natural laws.

Indeed, most of Shakespeare's plays are based on this same conflict, as are the themes in Plutarch, Dante, and Milton. In most of the old myths, epics, stories, and even histories, manmade laws and governments try to find a way around natural law. But they never quite succeed.

The overwhelming majority of humanity's great books and histories teach this same lesson: There are laws that are above humankind, and even humans' most powerful creations—governments—are bound by natural law.

> THE NATURAL LAW IS NOTHING ELSE THAN
> THE RATIONAL CREATURE'S PARTICIPATION IN THE ETERNAL LAW.
> —ST. THOMAS AQUINAS

The Lessons of Natural Law

Natural law has always existed, but the history of the human race's discovery of natural law is interesting. The great world religious writings, from the Bible to the Eastern Vedas, taught the importance of natural law, as mentioned earlier. Likewise, Plato and Aristotle were both concerned with natural law, specifically with the problem that arises in society when there is a difference between what is good and what is legal.[14]

Indeed, more recently, the famed Russian author Aleksandr Solzhenitsyn gave a speech at Harvard, where he addressed this very concern.[15] The timing of his speech in the late 1970s set the tone for his Cold War audience, who reportedly expected him (as a former political prisoner in the Soviet gulags) to criticize the communist model and praise the virtues of the American system. Solzhenitsyn did point out the ineffectiveness and even evils of the Soviet regime, but then he turned his attack on the American model. His biggest criticism, the reason he felt the Russian people should seek something much better than the American system to replace communism, was that in America, the culture—particularly in the political and corporate-industrial sectors of the economy—cares more about what is legal than what is right. This is precisely the kind of natural law concern Plato warned about.

Aristotle was long considered the "father of natural law"[16] because of his insistence that natural law exists and is real. But it was really Cicero who insisted that all human laws are only good or bad to the extent that they correspond to natural law.

Cicero's Contributions

Cicero noted that in all the tribes, cities, and nations around the known world, there were numerous systems of law and government. Some were effective, and others were not. Some laws and governing systems amounted to little more than the strong exerting force on the weak, while a few provided more freedom and opportunity for some or all of the people.

A few things are common to nearly all societies in history, including class divisions and the exploitation of the lower classes, widespread corruption in government, and some laws that don't follow common sense. But the surprising thing is that in the nations and societies where freedom and opportunity are widespread and lasting, a few key features are nearly always part of the legal and political system.

Obviously, these similarities seem likely to be rooted in some kind of natural, or higher, set of laws and principles. Cicero taught that reason was God's gift to man and that its main purpose was to allow humanity to understand and apply natural law. He wrote:

> True law is right reason in agreement with Nature; it is of universal application, unchanging and everlasting; it summons to duty by its commands, and averts from wrong-doing by its prohibitions.
>
> And it does not lay its commands or prohibitions upon good men in vain, though neither have any effect on the wicked. It is a sin to try to alter this law, nor is it allowable to attempt to repeal any part of it, and it is impossible to abolish it entirely.
>
> We cannot be freed from its obligations by Senate or People, and we need not look outside ourselves for an expounder or interpreter of it. And there will not be different laws at Rome and at Athens, or different laws now and in the future, but one

eternal and unchangeable law will be valid for all nations and for all times, and there will be one master and one ruler, that is, God, over us all, for He is the author of this law, its promulgator, and its enforcing judge.[17]

This provides an excellent overview of the nature and scope of natural law. In the ancient view of natural law, especially as espoused by the Stoics, the "notion of natural law clearly refers to . . . [a] contrast between 'nature' and 'convention.'"[18] Natural law, God's law, is lasting and natural, while manmade law is based on traditions, conventions, and the limited understandings of human beings.

This is significant because the "Roman jurists were a singularly unphilosophical breed of men."[19] They cared about laws that work, not about philosophy, theory, or ideals. Still, as the Roman professional class discovered, law that attempts to ignore or violate natural law ends up failing in the long term.[20]

Even those who didn't believe in God or any higher law frequently admitted that natural law works, though many of them simply explained this using the idea of "natural instinct."[21] Still, the existence of such a universal instinct led them to promote manmade laws that were careful not to violate natural law.

Some ancient jurists argued that no eternal law exists, but they still argued for the need of "justice," "equity," and laws that "correspond to nature."[22] Indeed, one of the most significant characteristics of natural law is its ability through history to convince people from incredibly diverse cultural traditions, backgrounds, and beliefs.

As stated above, people who want to remain free need to understand natural law. And part of this includes understanding the most important events in the history of humankind's discoveries of natural law.

Aquinas and Grotius

Another major contributor to natural law was the great Christian thinker St. Thomas Aquinas. He taught that the supreme laws of the universe are that there is a good, and that humanity's overarching commandment in this world is to do good.[23] The effective spread of this belief may be one of the most significant reasons for the rise of Western civilization to world power.

Compare this central operating principle ("your purpose is to do good in the world") that spread throughout the West to the top competing operating principles around the world ("your purpose is to serve the emperor, king, or caliph" or, alternatively, "your highest purpose is to get what you want for yourself"). The battles between these three views constitute an overview of world history.

Based on the teachings of Aquinas, "good is to be done; evil is to be avoided"[24] became the natural law maxim in the Middle Ages, and its influence remains today. Indeed, it is still the operating principle of both major Western political viewpoints: liberalism and conservatism. While progressives and conservatives sometimes disagree about exactly what is good and what is evil, the desire to do good and avoid evil remains foundational in both worldviews.

Aquinas also taught that manmade laws in conflict with natural laws are not actually laws but rather what he called "a corruption of law" and "an act of violence."[25] He further wrote, "Every human law has just so much of the nature of law as it is derived from the law of nature. But if in any point it departs from the law of nature, it is no longer a law but a perversion of law."[26]

In addition, Aquinas taught that, in at least one sense, God's law does something natural law cannot allow humankind to do. He said, "Man, the maker of human law, can pass judgment only upon external action, because man 'seeth those things that appear,' as we are told in the book of Kings. God alone, the divine Law-giver, is able to judge the inner movements of the will, as the psalmist said, 'The searcher of hearts and reins is God.'"[27]

The writer Hugo Grotius, who is also sometimes called the Father of Natural Law, focused on the existence of moral, natural, higher laws that nations should follow in their relations with each other. Some of these, such as the idea of the right to defend one's nation but not to engage in aggression or plunder for only political or financial gain, remain part of the modern worldview.

Again, this is all extremely relevant to the people in free nations because the government tends to operate as if it is the supreme being in the world and needs to get involved in every aspect of our lives. Natural law is a strong defense against this view of overreaching government, and in history, it is really the only view that has effectively kept government limited. Without the view of moral natural laws that are above humankind, every government eventually becomes far too big and controlling. And the only nations in history that have avoided such over-dominant government have been those where the common people understood natural law.

Such ideas may seem like mere philosophy to some people, but through history, all people who haven't understood natural law have lost their freedoms and prosperity to aristocrats, dictators, and elites.

John Locke and the Turning Point

It was John Locke who brought about the greatest historical turning point of humanity's appreciation for natural law. Locke argued that humanity should be ruled not by kings or the whims of aristocrats but rather by governments established under natural law and by the consent of the ordinary people in a society.

This set the stage for the American Revolution, the establishment of the US Constitution, and the spread of the ideas outlined in the Declaration of Independence, including the following:

- There are laws of nature and nature's God.

- These laws are above all manmade laws.

- All men are created equal.

- They are endowed by their Creator with inalienable rights.

- Government cannot legitimately take away these rights.

- Among these rights are life, liberty, property, and the pursuit of happiness.

- Governments are instituted to protect inalienable rights.

- At times, it is necessary for the people (not kings or aristocrats, but the masses) to change their government.

- The people have the right to alter or abolish government as they see fit.

- The people have the right to set up their government according to natural law.

- The people may set up their government as they see fit, as long as they follow natural law.

- Governments derive their legitimate powers from the consent of the people (not any one group, whether kings, scholars, priests, aristocrats, the wealthy, or those in power).

- It is the people's right and duty to ensure good government and to change it as needed.

All of this was a drastic departure from the governing views of the past, and each item on this list is based on the idea not only that natural law exists but that people and governments are bound by it. In short, the American founding was the greatest practical application of natural law views in recorded human history.

This was aided by the writings of Samuel Pufendorf, who was widely read by the American founding generation. Pufendorf taught that all laws should be based on natural law and outlined a whole system of practical government built upon natural laws, including such basics as property law and marriage and family law. Pufendorf's contributions were discussed in earlier chapters.

William Blackstone

The founders also leaned heavily on the writings of William Blackstone, who outlined the basics of English law on the principles of natural law. Blackstone collected the natural law philosophies of history into one place and outlined natural law's most important features.[28] For example, he taught that:

- Natural law governs the whole universe.

- Natural law includes revealed, scientific, moral, and political laws.

- Natural law is above humankind.

- All people in every nation and part of the world are subject to natural law whether they know about it or not.

- No human laws are valid if they conflict with natural law.

- Natural law is the supreme law over all other laws.

- Natural law is unchanging.

Blackstone's book came out in 1766 and was widely read and quoted by the founding generation along with the writings of Cicero, Pufendorf, and Locke, among others.

In short, if you remove the natural law principles of the American founding, nearly every important detail of the American freedom system—the Declaration, the Constitution, the political system, the protection of inalienable rights, the free enterprise economic model, and so forth—would disappear.

Blessings of Natural Law

Perhaps the greatest contribution of the natural law teachers was the idea that good laws are not those that are the most effectively enforced (despite the popularity of this definition among the ancient and medieval monarchs and aristocrats) but rather those that lead to increased morality and goodness among the leaders and people in a society. It was this idea that made natural law a topic of focus not only of jurists but for political philosophers, politicians, and officials—in ancient, medieval, and modern times.

From this perspective, the term "positive law" takes on a whole new meaning—not just law based on the positings of humankind, but law that truly creates a more positive world. Such positive law occurs where human laws and governments are most closely aligned with genuine natural law and universal truths.

In a world where natural law is widely understood, *ought* is more important than *must*, and "Is it good?" is much more sought after than merely "Is it legal?" The natural consequence of this change of human focus is to see the government as working for the people, rather than the people working for the government.

The point where law and morals intersected was the turning point in the history of freedom.[29] The natural law viewpoint (the idea that moral truths must govern the law and all manmade governments) changed everything. Over time, as understanding of natural law expanded, leaders, thinkers, and the people in free societies began to see law not as a set of aristocratic commands but rather as vital God-given protections of freedom. This was especially prevalent in the American founding, and in fact, the proliferation of ordinary people who understood the principles of natural law drastically changed the history of humanity. A world dominated by kings and aristocrats gave way to one where the people were seen as the true owners, holders, and overseers of freedom. This shift radically altered politics, economics, and society and ushered in the era known as modernity.

It permanently altered the course of history one otherwise normal day in April of 1775 when regular farmers stood firmly in fields near Lexington and Concord arrayed against soldiers clad in red and declared that governments belong to the people—not vice versa. And it came to a head on July 4, 1776, when the world heard the words, "We hold these truths to be self-evident…"

The Great Conversation

ENLIGHTENED STATESMEN WILL NOT ALWAYS BE AT THE HELM.
—JAMES MADISON, *FEDERALIST* 10

The Backlash

The ideas taught by Cicero, Aquinas, Pufendorf, Locke, and Blackstone—and applied by the American founders—were powerful, and they had a profound effect on many people around the world. Not surprisingly—given that the enemies of natural law were the most powerful, wealthy, and influential people in the world, especially the European monarchies and aristocracies—numerous attacks on natural law developed in the century after the American founding. The three most effective attacks on natural law were the ideas of relativism,[30] empiricism, and romanticism.[31]

Attack #1: Relativism

Relativism suggested that natural law is inadequate because it is too absolutist and that most real challenges in the legal and political world depend largely on the details of each specific situation. But even the most relativistic and situational ideas and events are still subject to guiding principles.

Relativism is too often used simply to support personal preferences,[32] and in reality, true relativism is the idea that different natural laws need to be used in different situations. Some critics of natural law have argued that every ideology uses the idea of natural law to support its own particular views,[33] but this is so widely attempted precisely because almost everyone accepts that there are, in fact, higher natural laws that are above human control.[34]

Attack #2: Empiricism

Empiricism argued that there are no tangible final proofs of any laws or lawgivers in the universe. With this worldview, how do we actually know that gravity is a law? It works here, on this earth, but have we tested it on all the other planets in existence? And until we do, how can we actually be sure that it is a universal law? By extension of such reasoning, if even the laws of science can't be proven infallible, then how can we be sure of any moral or political laws?

Empiricism doesn't refute the idea of natural law, but it argues that the existence of natural law cannot be absolutely proven and should therefore be doubted. Supporters of natural law respond by pointing out the historical record: When people have tried to circumvent natural law, they have failed. And only nations that have embraced natural law have created widespread opportunity, prosperity, and freedom for all.

Attack #3: Romanticism

Where both relativism and empiricism tried intellectual attacks, romanticism took a different approach. It couched law as the property of lawyers and government as the place for politicians.

The romantics never actually argued about the proper foundations of law or government. Instead, simply by popularizing the drama of attorneys and judges facing off in courtrooms and of politicians running for office and scrapping for power and influence despite all their personal flaws and enemies—and balancing it all with trying to maintain happy relationships with their families—they left the impression that ordinary people had no business in these circles.

The romanticist attack was successful to some extent, diminishing over time the deep passion people felt for frequent conversations about natural law and its impact on government and laws (as shown by the popular response of American farmers and merchants to the *Federalist* papers in the 1780s or to the Lincoln–Douglas debates in the 1850s).

Over time, empiricism and romanticism combined to convince most people that science, law, and government belong to the experts and that the rest of us should just leave such issues to specialists.

Political Parties

But even as this belief in reliance on experts—and the corresponding idea that the people should yield to specialists in matters of law and politics—spread in the modern free world, the traditions of the founding, rooted solidly in the principles of natural law, remained strong. Ironically, they were preserved, to a large extent, in the political parties.

Clearly, the political party system has its share of problems. But on the topic of natural law, both conservatives and liberals have helped preserve some of the most important principles of freedom and progress.

For example, natural law affirms that how we treat other people matters. It matters deeply. There is a natural law of right and wrong that governs all our relationships. Tolerance and inclusiveness, compassion and charity, fairness and individual liberty, anti-slavery, anti-racism, anti-bigotry, and a desire for progress are all foundational principles of liberalism. They are also all core values of natural law.

Likewise, the following conservative values are also natural laws: higher rewards for those who take risks; the rights of property and ownership; the commandments that thou shall not kill, steal, or commit adultery; self-reliance; justice for one's actions; the right to enjoy the fruits of one's successes; a proper role of government and the necessity of limiting government to its proper role; and freedom of opportunity but not of forced results.

Natural law is the basis of the best in both liberalism and conservatism, and the mistakes and flaws of both occur where natural law isn't consulted. Indeed, when the topic is natural law, the modern parties don't have much to disagree about. The problem is that one party champions a few natural laws, while the other emphasizes a different set of natural laws.

The Problem of Language

Moreover, the conflict can't be fixed when the conversations between parties take place almost exclusively in the languages of empiricism (science and academia) or romanticism (politics and law).

In other words, the way to get ahead in a career in science or academia is frequently to take a side and stick with it, and the same is often true in politics and law.

In contrast with the American founding era, the modern system itself doesn't encourage people from different parties to sit around and discuss natural law and how it can help us apply the best from both conservatism and liberalism. People can do it, if they choose, but where and when is it likely to happen? Most schools don't promote this kind of open dialogue, nor do businesses or media outlets. Cooperation doesn't sell as well as conflict.

And lawsuits and elections certainly aren't naturally suited for deep, important, good-faith conversations where all sides are sincerely trying to learn from one another.

Community Matters

Unfortunately, as the twentieth century progressed, our institutions lost their normal natural law environment, and it was replaced with empirical and romanticist events and systems. For example, consider the old television show *Little House on the Prairie.* For much of America's history, adults met each Sunday in a setting ideally suited to learn other views beyond their own, and they did the same at least one night a week in a town meeting where all adults were in attendance.

The Norman Rockwell painting of a man speaking at a civic event is indicative of this history. Robert Putnam's important book *Bowling Alone: The Collapse and Revival of American Community* discusses how in the 1950s and 1960s, America was unofficially organized into deeply connected communities based around civic and church groups, bowling teams, sports fans, work groups meeting socially (e.g., fire fighters or police officers from a certain precinct and their families), fraternal clubs, and so forth.

In recent decades, people are more likely to bowl, dine, go to the movies, worship, or even fire up the grill on the patio alone—or with just members of their immediate family. Unfortunately, the revival of community that Putnam hoped was occurring has turned out to be almost exclusively limited to online communities. In all this, people tend to listen only to the views of others who agree with them—politically, religiously, and at the same socioeconomic level.

There are, of course, exceptions to this depressing trend, but they are few. Most people have the habit of viewing society from a specific, inflexible viewpoint, and they are leery of reaching out or trying to connect with others from different perspectives.

The result is that we are a society deeply divided into isolated cliques. We rub shoulders with an incredibly diverse group of people as we shop, drive, attend school, seek entertainment, and even work. But we talk about deep ideas very little and listen even less to ideas that are different from our own.

Allan Bloom wrote in *The Closing of the American Mind* that even families have this divide: "People sup together, play together, travel together, but they do not think together. Hardly any homes have any intellectual life whatsoever, let alone one that informs the vital interests of life. Educational TV marks the high tide of family intellectual life."[35]

If even families face such challenges, and many do, imagine how wide the divide is in broader society. As an example, when was the last time you had a long talk with someone of a different religion where you sincerely tried to understand them and even affirm them for their choices? When was the last time you spent time socially with people who deeply disagree with your political views and took the time to truly listen to their viewpoint and openly learn from their ideas? Or when was the last time you spent a day with someone from a totally different career field and economic class than you, just talking pleasantly and equitably about important issues of law and government?

We are a diverse generation in some ways, but we are also deeply divided. And how can we heal these divisions if we don't sit together, eat together, talk together, and genuinely listen to those who are different?

The Need

We need natural law and the common language it brings. It is the root of modern freedom and the foundation of both major political philosophies in the free world. It allows us to talk together, but we have to be willing to listen and genuinely learn.

Natural law is real. There are laws that are above humankind. History is clear on this point: Humankind can try to break the natural political laws—for example, it can engage in slavery or violent aggression—but such violations of natural law always bring negative consequences. Human governments are subject to the laws of nature.

Of course, it is impossible to forget that bad laws, or even "a society founded on evil laws," may not have the support of the people but can still maintain power by the use of force and violence.[36] Indeed, this is the history of most governments over time. But while manmade law is important, and often very powerful, it is not supreme. It is only good if it adheres to natural law, and when it breaks natural law, it is no better than rules agreed to by a band of thieves.[37]

Natural law is supreme, and all success and progress come from properly following and applying true principles of natural law. This is true in business, as taught by such greats as Napoleon Hill, David Schwartz, James Allen, Zig Ziglar, George Clason, Earl Nightingale, Dennis Deaton, Stephen Covey, and others. It is the basis of success in every field, from family to career to government.

Natural laws are the supreme laws, and societies that understand and apply natural law are consistently free, prosperous, and happy. The direction of any society, whether it is headed toward increased opportunity and freedom or their decline, indicates how closely it is focused on applying natural law. The same is true of any individual, family, business, or community.

Success and progress are the direct and inevitable consequence of properly applying natural laws. This is true of people, and it is true for governments and nations as well. Without adherence to natural law, our nations will fail.

RECOMMENDED READINGS ON NATURAL LAW

Talmud
Psalms 36–37; 118–119
Proverbs 8
Romans 2
Genesis 9; 17; 26
Exodus 12–13; 20–31; 34–35; 40
Deuteronomy 1; 4–27; 30
Joshua 1; 8; 22
Matthew 5–7; 16; 18; 22
Luke 6; 10; 22
John 3; 6; 13–17
Romans 3–13
1 Corinthians 11–34
Galatians 3–6
Hebrews 7–10

Sophocles, *Antigone*
Aeschylus, *Seven Against Thebes*
Euripedes, *Phoenician Maidens*
Plato, *Seventh Letter, Republic, Crito, Apology*
Aristotle, *Politics, Ethics*
Cicero, *Republic, Laws*
Aurelius, *Meditations*
Augustine, *City of God, Confessions*
Plutarch, *Lives*

Aquinas, *Summa Theologica*
Dante, *Divine Comedy*
Luther, *A Treatise on Christian Liberty*
Calvin, *Institutes of the Christian Religion*

Suárez, *Selections from Three Works of Francisco Suárez*
Shakespeare, *Troilus and Cressida, Hamlet, Macbeth*
Bacon, *Advancement of Learning*
Cervantes, *Don Quixote*
Milton, *Paradise Lost*
Smith, *The Wealth of Nations*
Gibbon, *Decline and Fall of the Roman Empire*

Turnbull, *Principles of Moral and Christian Philosophy*
Montesquieu, *Spirit of the Laws*
Locke, *Human Understanding, Civil Government*
Coke, *Institutes of the Laws of England*
Grotius, *The Rights of War and Peace*
Pufendorf, *On the Law of Nature and Nations, Two Books of the Elements of Universal Jurisprudence, Whole Duty of Man According to the Law of Nature*
Blackstone, *Commentaries on the Laws of England*
Vattel, *The Law of Nations*
Cumberland, *Treatise of the Laws of Nature*
Declaration of Independence
Paine, *Rights of Man*
Articles of Confederation
Constitution of the United States
The Federalist
Adams, *Discourses on Davila, Thoughts on Governments*
Tucker, *View of the Constitution of the United States*
Burke, *Reflections on the Revolution in France*
Millar, *An Historical View of the English Government*
Mill, *Utilitarianism*
Dickens, *A Tale of Two Cities, Pickwick Papers*

Tocqueville, *Democracy in America*

Bastiat, *Selected Essays on Political Economy, Economic Sophisms, Economic Harmonies*

Thoreau, *Civil Disobedience*

Emerson, *Essay on Self-Reliance*

Acton, *Essays on Freedom and Power*

Bryce, *The American Commonwealth*

Corwin, *The "Higher Law" Background of American Constitutional Law*

Mises, *The Ultimate Foundation of the Economic Science*

Strauss, *Natural Right and History*

Solzhenitsyn, *A World Split Apart*

Skousen, *The Five Thousand Year Leap, The Making of America*

Bolt, *A Man for All Seasons*

Bloom, *The Closing of the American Mind*

Brady, *PAiLS*

Budziszewski, *Written on the Heart*

Damon, *Noble Purpose*

DeMille, *1913, FreedomShift, The Coming Aristocracy*

Hyneman and Lutz, *American Political Writing during the Founding Era*

Palmer, *Uncommon Sense*

Sandoz, *Political Sermons of the American Founding Era, The Roots of Liberty*

Woodward, *RESOLVED*

NOTES

Chapter 1: The Law of Supremacy

1. Marcus Tullius Cicero, quoted in William Ebenstein, *Great Political Thinkers* (Stamford, CT: Cengage Learning, 1963), 134–135.
2. See *Gibbons v. Ogden* (1824).
3. Alexander Hamilton, *Federalist* 31, 78. See commentary in Hadley Arkes, "The Natural Law Challenge," *Harvard Journal of Law and Public Policy* (Summer 2013): 961–975.
4. See, for example, George Washington, letter to Bryan Fairfax, August 24, 1774; John Adams, "A Defence of the Constitutions of the Government of the United States of America," in *The Political Writings of John Adams*, ed. George W. Carey (Washington, DC: Regnery, 2000) 301; Alexander Hamilton, *Federalist* 31, 78; *Calder v. Bull* (1798).

Chapter 2: The Law of Authority

1. Cited in Paul E. Sigmund, *Natural Law in Political Thought* (Cambridge, MA: Winthrop, 1971), 57.
2. Pufendorf taught that natural law has three major divisions: (1) how we should behave toward God and nature, (2) how we should behave toward ourselves and morality, and (3) how we should behave toward others. His commentary on natural law and its relationship to manmade government comes in the third part of natural law, or "how we should behave toward others." In this discussion, Pufendorf started at the beginning of manmade laws and outlined what natural law expects of human governments and laws. Samuel von Pufendorf, *The Whole Duty of Man According to the Law of Nature* (Charleston,

SC: Forgotten Books, 2012, facsimile of the 1735 R. Gosling publication), 42.

3. John Locke showed the flaws of this perspective in *Two Essays of Government,* which was widely read in the American colonies.

4. Pufendorf, 89–109, 196–201, 218–225.

5. Ibid.

6. Ibid.

7. The Declaration of Independence.

Chapter 3: The Law of Limits

1. *Federalist* 1, 10, 14, 51.

2. *Federalist* 1.

3. See, for example, *Federalist* 18–20.

4. *Federalist* 47–51, 53, 60.

5. W. Cleon Skousen, *The Five Thousand Year Leap* (Washington, DC: National Center for Constitutional Studies, 1981), 15–19.

6. Ibid.

7. Pufendorf, 207.

8. See Adrienne Koch, *The American Enlightenment* (New York: Braziller, 1965), 239.

9. Alexis de Tocqueville, *Democracy in America*, vol. 1 (New York: Vintage Books, 1945), 329.

Chapter 4: The Law of Delegation

1. Cited in Sigmund, 58.

2. Pufendorf, 95–99.

Chapter 5: The Law of Force

1. Frédéric Bastiat, *The Law* (1850) (New York: Foundation for Economic Education, 1995), 51.

2. Consider the following definition of the word *government* from *Black's Law Dictionary*: "The regulation, restraint, supervision, or control which is exercised upon the individual members of an organized . . . society by those invested with authority; or the act of exercising supreme political power or control" (Henry Campbell Black, ed., *Black's Law Dictionary*, 6th ed. (Eagan, MN: West, 1990), 695.

3. See C. S. Lewis, *The Abolition of Man* (New York: HarperCollins, 1944).

4. Bastiat, 51.

5. Ibid., 52.

6. Leo Strauss, *Natural Right and History* (Chicago: University of Chicago Press, 1965), 235.

7. Bastiat, 94–96.

8. Ibid., 52.

9. Ibid., 53.

10. Ibid., 61–65.

11. Ibid.

12. Ibid., 65.

Chapter 6: The Law of Decline

1. Bastiat, 65.

2. Ibid.

3. Ibid., p. 64.

4. Ibid., 56–66.

5. Ibid., 61.

6. Ibid.

7. Ibid.

Chapter 7: The Law of Power

1. Frédéric Bastiat, 1850, "What Is Seen and What Is Not Seen," in *Selected Essays on Political Economy*.

Chapter 8: The Law of Gaps

1. See Oliver DeMille, *1913* (Flint, MI: Obstaclés, 2012), chs. 1–6.

Chapter 9: The Law of the Vital Few

1. Phil Cooke, *One Big Thing* (Nashville: Thomas Nelson, 2012), 33.

2. Cited in ibid., 8.

3. Cited in ibid., 34.

4. For a further discussion of mini-factories, see Oliver DeMille, *The Coming Aristocracy* (Center for Social Leadership, 2009).

5. See Jonathan Hughes, *The Vital Few* (New York: Oxford University Press, 1966).

Chapter 10: The Law of Liberty

1. Cited in Sigmund, 102.
2. Note that there is disagreement about the way this has been quoted and translated over time, and many believe that in the original source there were only four stanzas, not five, and that the fourth stanza in the longer version included here was added later and not part of the original.

Chapter 11: The Law of Economy

1. *Federalist* 51.
2. Ibid.
3. Thomas Jefferson, *Writings of Thomas Jefferson*, Albert Ellery Bergh, ed., vol. 14, page 421, cited in Skousen, 238.
4. Ibid.
5. John Fiske, 1916, *The Critical Period of American History, 1783-1789*, volume 12, pages 282–283, cited in Skousen, 240.

Appendix: A Brief History of Natural Law

1. Mortimer J. Adler, ed., *The Great Ideas: A Syntopicon*, vol. 2 (Encyclopedia Brittanica, 1990), 964.
2. See Heinrich A. Rommen, *The Natural Law* (Indianapolis: Liberty Fund, 1998), xx.
3. See A. P. d'Entrèves, *Natural Law* (n.c.: Hutchinson University Library edition, 1951), 175.
4. Adler, 963.
5. Cited in ibid., 967.
6. Ibid.
7. Sophocles, *Antigone.*
8. Sigmund, 1.
9. Ibid.
10. Ibid.
11. Ibid., 3.
12. Plato, *Protagoras.* See further commentary in Sigmund, 3–4.
13. Plato, *Gorgias* and *The Republic.* See further commentary in Sigmund, 4–5.
14. Ibid., 11–14.

15. Aleksandr Solzhenitsyn, *A World Split Apart* (New York: HarperCollins, 1978).

16. Rommen, 14.

17. Cited in d'Entrèves, 25.

18. d'Entrèves, 27.

19. Ibid., 28.

20. Ibid.

21. Ibid., 32.

22. Ibid., 35.

23. Ibid., 42–43.

24. Ibid., 45–47.

25. Cited in Sigmund, 45.

26. Cited in Adler, 968.

27. From the *Summa Theologica*, cited in d'Entrèves, 86.

28. William Blackstone, 1766, *Commentaries on the Laws of England* 1766, vol. 1 (Chicago: University of Chicago Press, 1979).

29. See d'Entrèves, 116.

30. Sigmund, ix.

31. Rommen, 99–105.

32. See Sigmund, 208.

33. See Sigmund, 207.

34. See Sigmund, 212–213.

35. Allan Bloom, *The Closing of the American Mind* (New York: Simon and Schuster, 1987), 58.

36. D'Entrèves, 199.

37. Cited in Ebenstein, 134–135.

Oliver DeMille is a *New York Times, Wall Street Journal,* and *USA Today* bestselling author and a popular keynote speaker. He is the author or coauthor of *Leadership Education, FreedomShift, The Coming Aristocracy, 1913, The Student Whisperer,* and *LeaderShift.* He is also the founder of the Thomas Jefferson Education (TJEd) style of learning and a founder of The Center for Social Leadership. Oliver and his wife Rachel have eight children.

Connect with Oliver at oliverdemille.com
and on Facebook, Twitter, and LinkedIn